Sparky Smart

FROM PRIORY PARK

THE Crinkly Cousins
AND OTHER MISHAPS

WRITTEN BY
ALEXA TEWKESBURY
ILLUSTRATED BY
ANNA-MARIA GLOVER

kevin mayhew

kevin mayhew

First Published in 2023 by Kevin Mayhew Ltd

Kevin Mayhew Ltd
Fengate Farm
Rattlesden
Bury St Edmunds
Suffolk
IP30 0SZ

Sparky Smart written by Alexa Tewkesbury
Illustrated by Anna-Maria Glover

ISBN 9781838581497
Product code: 1501722

Meet the family!

Sparky (Sabrina)

Mr Smart (Seb/Dad)

Mrs Smart (Stella/Mum)

Stanley

Sissy

THE BAGGS

Auntie Bella (Stella's twin sister)
The twins: Nat and Archie (aka 'the crinkly cousins')
Grandad Bagg (Stella and Auntie Bella's dad)

RESIDENTS OF PRIORY PARK

Miss Clatworthy
Her cats:
Monday, Tuesday
and Thursday

The Obis
Mr Obi
Mrs Obi
Baby Eric
Minnie,
the Chihuahua

The crinkly cousins come to stay

BANG!

The car door slammed so hard outside the house that the window of Stanley Smart's bedroom shook.

Well, it didn't really. But Stanley always liked to exaggerate when he was annoyed.

'Did you feel that?' hollered Stanley, as he stormed out onto the landing.

'Feel what?' His sister, Sparky, was busy sticking pressed leaves onto her bedroom door with sticky-tack.

'*That!* The window in my bedroom shook when those kids slammed the car door!'

'No, it didn't.'

Sparky was used to her brother's bad moods when their cousins came to stay. At 13, he was three years older than they were. Having them around for more than an hour at a time was just annoying.

They had whiney voices.

They didn't always wash their hands before meals (Stanley was a stickler for clean hands).

And they mostly forgot to take off their shoes when they came through the front door.

Not only that, whenever they stayed, Stanley's bedroom was no longer his own.

Mr Smart would pump up two blow-up mattresses for the cousins to sleep on. Then, he'd lie the mattresses side by side on the floor, jammed between Stanley's bed and his wardrobe. In fact, the only way Stanley could then get to his bed was to clamber over the mattresses. And as for opening his wardrobe door, it was easier just to wear the same clothes until his cousins went home again.

'It did,' Stanley insisted. '**Bam!**' He mimed slamming a car door. 'The whole house totally shook!'

'It didn't.' Sparky tossed her sandy-coloured plaits

car door and the whole house shook.'

He turned and stomped back into his bedroom.

Sparky shrugged her shoulders. 'No, it didn't.'

Sparky knew she was right. She was quite often right. Even her teacher, Mrs Primrose, had said so in Sparky's school report: 'Whenever I ask a question, Sabrina's hand is always one of the first to shoot up. Her answers are quite often right too. Even when they're not, she gives her wrong answers very enthusiastically.'

Sparky often thought about that report – the part about her right answers, anyway. She chose to quietly forget the part about her wrong answers. Mrs Primrose had said she was 'quite often right' and that's what mattered. Anyway, you don't get to be called 'Sparky' for no good reason.

Actually, there was a very good reason. But it had nothing to do with being quite often right.

Sparky's real name was Sabrina. When she was little, she was determined to be in charge.

If Mrs Smart took little Sabrina and Stanley to the park, Sabrina would never allow Stanley to push her on the swings. 'No!' little Sabrina would say. 'I want to push Stanley.' And she did.

If Mrs Smart took her to paddle in the stream, little Sabrina would refuse to wear her wellies. 'Nasty wellies,' she would say. 'Want bare toesies.' And she would kick her wellies off and jump in the water before Mrs Smart could stop her.

When little Sabrina started school, she was the one who would take other children to the toilet if they were too scared to go by themselves. And whenever her teacher needed something fetched or carried, little Sabrina would grab it before the rest of the class had a chance to blink.

'Well,' her teacher had said to Mrs Smart at the end of her first week, '**she's certainly a sparky one**.'

So that's how it happened. Little Sabrina Smart became known as Little Miss Sparky. And, even though she was nearly nine now, the Sparky part had stuck.

The front doorbell rang.

'I don't know why they're ringing the bell,' Stanley's voice continued to grumble through his open doorway. 'We all know they're here. When they slammed the car door the whole house shook.'

Sparky scampered downstairs.

Stanley's caterpillars bumped heads again. 'What about your leaves?'

'What about them?' Sparky replied.

'Nat! Archie!' Mrs Smart just beat Sparky to the door. She flung it wide and gave the twins a big, beaming smile. She also gave them each a big hug. They hated that. Mrs Smart knew they hated it. They always stood stiffly, arms clamped to their sides. But Mrs Smart made a point of hugging them anyway. It wasn't entirely easy today. She had her youngest, two-year-old Sissy, clutched to her hip at the same time.

'Look at you two! I'm sure you've grown a few inches since we last saw you.'

This was something Mrs Smart said whenever she saw the twins. And as she saw them quite often, they probably wouldn't have had time to grow that much.

'But thank goodness you've still got your gorgeous

curly hair.'

Archie raised an eyebrow. 'Crinkly,' he corrected.

'Sorry?' said Mrs Smart.

'It's crinkly hair,' said Sparky, 'not curly hair. We had this conversation last time they came to stay. And the time before. Curly hair curls and crinkly hair crinkles. And Nat and Archie's hair definitely crinkles.'

'Does it?' Mrs Smart glanced at the tops of the boys' heads. 'Oh, of course it does. Silly me. Sorry – it's been a *long* term.'

If ever Mrs Smart forgot anything, she blamed her job. She was a maths teacher. A maths teacher in a secondary school.

As well as making her forgetful, being a maths teacher in a secondary school also apparently made her lose her keys (quite often), burn dinner (sometimes), call Sparky 'Stanley' and Stanley 'Sparky' (very occasionally), and run out of petrol (once). It also meant that she frequently woke up in a bad mood – especially on Monday mornings.

'**Stanley!**' Mrs Smart suddenly turned away to call up the stairs. 'Stanley, come down and say hello to Nat and Archie. Anyway' – turning back to the boys – 'don't just stand there, come on in.'

Mrs Smart hardly needed to give the invitation. Just as she did so, the boys' mum jogged over from the car purposefully. So purposefully, in fact, that she ran into them and practically knocked them through the doorway and into the house.

Bella Bagg was something of a whirlwind. She was divorced and seemed to think she had to do everything at 90 miles an hour – her job, the cleaning, the washing, the cooking, even the school run. She'd decided that, as a single parent, she obviously had twice as much to do as two parents. Therefore she needed to do everything at least twice as quickly.

Mrs Smart (whose name was Stella) and Auntie Bella were twins like Nat and Archie. Their mother had thought it would be fun to give them names that rhymed – so, Stella and Bella. It hadn't been much fun at all. While they were growing up, it was just horribly confusing.

'I don't know which one of you it was that slammed the car door,' Auntie Bella said, her eyes darting from Nat to Archie and back again, 'but I'm sure the house shook – didn't it, Auntie Stella?'

Stanley had appeared at the top of the stairs, a sulky look on his face. It vanished for a moment behind a smug smile as he heard Auntie Bella's words. Good old Auntie Bella. However much Stanley might feel a bit of a misfit in his family from time to time, he and his auntie? They understood each other.

Auntie Bella dragged the suitcase she was pulling through the front doorway. The case had a wonky wheel which made dragging it anywhere a bit of a chore. Today, the wonky wheel got caught on the threshold. Rather than having a look to see where and how it was caught, Auntie Bella simply wrenched at the suitcase handle.

The case ended up successfully in the hall.

The wonky wheel, however, remained on the doorstep.

Auntie Bella glanced at it. 'Oh,' she said.

'Can you stop for a cup of tea?' asked Mrs Smart.

'Gosh, no,' said Auntie Bella. 'I've got work coming out of my eyeballs.'

Sparky looked at her. She tried to picture Auntie Bella's work being squeezed out through her eyes... Interesting...

Auntie Bella worked for a magazine. She wrote about this, that and the other. She interviewed local celebrities. She was given free tickets for things like choir concerts and scone-baking contests.

Sparky thought it sounded exciting and glamorous. She wanted to be a writer when she grew up. But Auntie Bella wished she didn't have to go to work at all.

'Not even a quick one?' said Mrs Smart. She sounded disappointed.

'Not even a quick one, I'm afraid,' said Auntie Bella. 'I've got four stories to write up for Monday morning, including one about a pianist who broke her arm but went ahead with her concert anyway. Well, it *was* for charity, so good for her, that's what I say. And I've got no food in the house, the washing machine's on the blink, and it's going to take me at least an hour to get home.'

'Right,' said Mrs Smart.

'Bye then, boys,' said Auntie Bella. 'Love you lots. Be good for Auntie Stella.' She gave them both a quick kiss.

'And lots of love to all of you too,' she added. She blew kisses to Sparky, and to Stanley who still stood at the top of the stairs, and patted little Sissy on the head. 'Sorry to dash, Stella, but you know how it is. See you all on Friday. Byeee!'

Auntie Bella swept out through the front door, one hand raised, fingers waggling in a 'goodbye' sort of gesture.

For a few seconds, the house was suddenly very still.

And very quiet.

Then there was the slam of a car door and the sound of the engine starting (on the fourth go).

And Auntie Bella screeched away.

Mrs Smart reached out and shoved the front door shut. Sparky's foot nearly got caught as it swung closed, but she just managed to jump out of the way in time. You see, not only was Sparky quite often right, she was also very quick-thinking. Which (being part of the Smart family), she'd discovered was just as well.

Should she remind her mum about the wonky wheel on the front step, she wondered?

'Right,' Mrs Smart said again. '*I'm* going to have a cup of tea. Who's for some squash?'

'What flavour?' asked Archie.

'Yes, please,' said Nat. 'Are there any biscuits?'

'Stosh,' said Sissy.

As Mrs Smart went into the kitchen, she called to Stanley, 'Stanley, do come down. In fact, what would be really helpful is if you could carry the boys' suitcase up to your room. Now then, where's that kettle...?'

Two hours after tea and squash and biscuits – not to mention the chocolate cake that Nat found in a red-and-white spotted tin on the kitchen bench – Mrs Smart had dinner on the table. To be honest, no one really wanted any dinner after all the biscuits and chocolate cake. But it was dinner time and Sissy needed to be put to bed soon.

Archie eyed his peas suspiciously.

'Are these frozen peas or are they out of a tin?' he asked.

Sparky stopped eating, her fork halfway to her mouth.

Mrs Smart sat next to Sissy at the other end of the table. Sparky glanced in their direction, and waited for Mrs Smart's eye to twitch.

The eye twitch was something odd that happened sometimes when Mrs Smart was annoyed. Sparky and Stanley found it quite useful. If they were arguing, for instance, and happened to spot a twitch of Mrs Smart's eye, they knew it was a good time to stop. As it didn't always happen, however, sometimes they didn't stop until it was too late.

Little Sissy was busy spooning her peas off her plate and onto the table. Mrs Smart was busy spooning them back onto Sissy's plate again. At Archie's question, she stopped, and her eye began to twitch at once – in the twinkling of an eye, you might say.

Oops, thought Sparky.

It wasn't that Mrs Smart was especially impatient. But Archie was an especially fussy eater. The Smarts knew this only too well from all the times the twins had come to stay.

Mrs Smart drew in a breath. 'Actually, Archie,' she said, 'they're not frozen and they're not out of a tin either. They're fresh peas, Archie. Fresh out of their pods from next door's garden.'

Archie looked confused. In the whole of his ten years, he'd never come across a 'fresh' pea. Peas either came out of a bag from the freezer, rock hard and covered in frost; or they came from a tin – all sickly green and squidgy, and definitely the most disgusting things ever to end up on his plate.

But *fresh* peas? How was that even possible?

'What do you mean – fresh?' asked Archie. He picked up his fork and started poking and prodding at the peas in front of him.

Mrs Smart's eye began to twitch faster.

'Where do you think peas come from, Archie?' Sparky said. 'Before they end up in the freezer or in tins?'

Archie looked at her as if he didn't understand the question.

'Peas are a vegetable, Archie, didn't you know?' said Sparky. 'They grow on plants. Our neighbours grow loads of vegetables. They quite often give us things when they've got too much.'

Archie looked put out. 'Of course I know peas are vegetables,' he said.

'He probably didn't,' said Nat. 'He hardly ever eats vegetables, so how would he know what they are?'

'I *do so* know what a vegetable is!' Archie said. 'Cabbages are vegetables. And carrots. So are tomatoes.'

'Well, strictly speaking,' corrected Sparky, 'a tomato is a fruit.'

'No, it's not,' said Archie. 'How can a tomato be a fruit?'

'It just is,' said Sparky.

Archie shook his head. 'No, it's not. A banana's a fruit. Or an apple. Or a peach. You have peaches and ice cream, don't you? Whoever heard of tomatoes and ice cream?'

Sparky shrugged. 'They're still a fruit.'

'No, they're not,' said Archie.

'Are,' said Sparky.

'Aren't,' said Archie.

'Are.'

'Aren't!'

'Oh, who cares what they are?' interrupted Stanley. *Is every dinner time going to be like this from now until next Friday?* he wondered. 'Peas are vegetables, Archie. They grow on plants. In pods. They're good for you, you should eat them.'

Mrs Smart had had enough. She was losing the pea-on-the-plate battle with Sissy. Having a different kind of pea battle with Archie didn't interest her one little bit. Not only that, her own peas were going cold.

'If you don't want your peas, Archie,' she said, 'then don't eat them. But please do try to eat everything else.'

There was silence for a moment.

With his knife, very carefully, Archie slid his peas to one side.

Everyone watched.

They kept on watching as Archie inspected everything else on his plate. He was just about to load up his fork with mashed potato when he stopped.

He pointed.

'Is this fish finger cod or haddock?'

Suddenly, there was a loud **THUD**, as if something had fallen hard against the front door. This was followed a few moments later by the much quieter sound of a key turning in the lock.

Mr Smart's voice sailed through the hall into the kitchen, 'What's this wonky wheel doing on the door step? I just went flying!'

Stanley had a favourite place to sit in the lounge. It was at the left end of the big sofa, next to the radiator. In winter, he could rest his feet on the radiator, so his toes were always as warm as toast when he was watching TV. (They would also have been as warm as toast if he'd worn his slippers. But Stanley always forgot that he had slippers.)

The left end of the big sofa was Stanley's. All the Smart family knew it. Well, except little Sissy. But she was still small enough for Stanley to pick her up and put her back down again at the right end.

Even Mr and Mrs Obi next door knew about Stanley and the left end of the big sofa. So when they visited, they always sat very politely on the small sofa under the window.

Yes, Stanley and his sofa seat were not to be messed with.

So it's a shame, Stanley always thought, *that not one single member of his family had bothered to explain this to Nat and Archie.*

That evening, Nat sat at the left end of the big sofa. Sparky sat next to him, and Archie perched beside her at the other end.

Stanley could have sat on the sofa under the window, but he didn't. He sat on the floor to make a point, and leant his back against the radiator. This was extremely uncomfortable. It was cold, too, because the radiator was off.

'So,' said Nat. 'What are we doing tomorrow?'

'It's Sunday,' said Sparky. 'We're going to church.'

'What?' Nat said. He made a face. 'We did that last

time we were here on a Sunday. And the time before. Can't we do something else?'

'Why don't you want to go to church?' asked Sparky.

'I don't *not* want to go to church. **I just thought we could do something different.**'

'Like what?' Sparky said.

'*I* don't know.' Nat leaned forward. 'Arch, what could we do?'

Archie was digging around in his mouth with his finger. Something was caught between his teeth and he was trying to get it out. He suspected it was some pea skin. He'd eaten a pea by mistake when it got mixed up with his mashed potato.

He shrugged his shoulders. 'Gon asch gee, I gunno...' he mumbled through his digging finger. Which could have meant anything.

'Well...' Nat flopped back against the cushion.

That's MY cushion Nat's flopping all over, thought Stanley. *Because he's in MY seat.*

Nat continued re-planning the day. 'We could... we could... go to the park?'

'We could,' agreed Sparky. 'Except it's not very nice down there at the moment. They're re-wotsitting it.'

Nat frowned. 'Re-what-ing it?'

'You know,' said Sparky. 'They're putting down a new... thingy.'

'What's a thingy?'

'Oh, come on, Nat, you know,' replied Sparky. 'A thingy – a wotsit.' As she spoke, Sparky flapped her hands in the air.

'Something to do with butterflies?' Archie suggested helpfully. He'd removed his finger from his mouth and was inspecting his fingernail for signs of pea skin.

Sparky looked at him. 'Why would it have anything to do with butterflies?' she asked.

'What Sparky's trying to tell you – and doing a really bad job of it,' Stanley said, 'is that they're resurfacing the car park and the tennis courts down there. So it's all a right mess. And it stinks of tar.'

'Oh.' Nat took this in. 'I quite like the smell of tar,' he said.

'That's because you're weird,' said Archie.

And a sofa stealer, thought Stanley.

Archie's finger returned to poking about in his mouth.

Nat said, 'Well, there must be somewhere else... I know! We could go ice skating!'

Sparky shook her head. 'The skating rink's not there anymore.'

'What do you mean? Why?' Nat used his whiney voice. The whiney voice that Stanley hated.

'I don't know,' said Sparky. 'Maybe the ice melted. It has been quite warm.'

Stanley was going to argue that the ice wouldn't have melted because it was warm. There were special machines to keep it frozen. He knew this because he was very interested in how things worked.

At the moment, Stanley was especially interested in how the weather worked. So interested, in fact, that he had decided he was going to be a weather person on the TV when he grew up.

But before he could open his mouth, Mrs Smart walked in.

'Good,' she said. 'That's Sissy off to bed. Now, boys, shall we get your sleeping bags sorted out?'

'Mum?' said Sparky.

'Yes, Sparky,' said Mrs Smart.

'Nat says he doesn't want to go to church tomorrow.'

'Oh?' Mrs Smart glanced at Nat.

'So, what I was wondering was,' Sparky continued, 'why don't you all go, and Nat and I can stay here.'

'Why?' said Mrs Smart. 'Don't you want to go either?'

'Yes, of course *I* want to go,' Sparky replied. 'We're making a collage of things we're thankful for and I'm taking in leaves because I'm thankful for trees. But if Nat doesn't want to go, I don't mind staying at home with him. It's only for one Sunday.'

Mrs Smart folded her arms. 'How old are you, Sparky?' she said.

Strange question. Aren't mums supposed to know that sort of thing about their children?

'Erm... eight,' said Sparky.

'**Exactly,**' said Mrs Smart. '**You're eight years old**. Responsible parents do not leave their eight-year-olds at home on their own.'

'But I won't be on my own, will I? I'll be with Nat.'

Mrs Smart blinked. 'Sweetheart, Nat's only nine. Responsible aunties don't leave their nine-year-old nephews at home on their own either. And before you say' – and Mrs Smart held up her hands – 'that he won't be on his own, he'll be with you, neither of you is old enough to be left here alone. With or without each other. So, I'm sorry, but we're all going to church.'

'Actually,' said Nat, 'I'm ten.'

Mrs Smart looked at him. 'Pardon?'

'Arch and me,' Nat said. 'We're ten.'

'We're ten, yeah,' said Archie.

'When did that happen?' Mrs Smart looked quite put out.

'Well...' Nat hesitated. Was this a trick question? 'On our birthday.'

'You remember, Mum,' said Sparky. 'Last month. Dad wanted to buy them proper running shorts, but Nat hates running. So we got them both inflatable dinosaurs instead.'

'Yes, of course I remember *that*,' said Mrs Smart. Her eye was just short of twitching. 'But I could have sworn you turned nine.'

'Nope,' said Archie. 'That was last year.'

'Oh.' Mrs Smart frowned. She looked as if she was trying to do adding-up sums in her head.

'Don't worry, Mum,' said Sparky. 'You can't be expected to remember everything. After all, it has been a *very* long term.'

Mrs Smart stopped doing sums in her head and looked hard at her daughter. 'Anyway,' she said, 'we'll go to church in the morning. You'll love it, boys, you'll see. I think the drama group might be doing something again – they're always funny. And if they ask for volunteers, you could give it a go like you did last time you were here. You were seeds, I think, when they did the Parable of the Sower... Or were you weeds...?' She shook her head. 'Well, you were seeds or weeds, I'm sure you were, and you were absolutely brilliant.'

No one said a word.

'Good,' said Mrs Smart. '**That's settled then.**'

She was about to head for the kitchen to make herself a cup of tea when Sparky said, 'Mum?'

'Yes, Sparky,' said Mrs Smart.

'If I'm eight,' said Sparky, 'and Nat's ten, then eight plus ten makes eighteen. Doesn't it?'

Mrs Smart's eyes narrowed slightly. 'Yes, Sparky,' she said.

'That means,' Sparky continued, 'that Nat and my ages combined makes eighteen. So *that* means that, both together, we're eighteen years old. And responsible parents and aunties wouldn't mind leaving their eighteen-year-olds at home on their own – would they?'

Mrs Smart's eye twitched once. Then twice.

'Sabrina,' she said, 'I'm going to the kitchen now to make a cup of tea. Don't follow me.'

And she left the room.

⁂ ⁂ ⁂ ⁂

When the Smarts sat down to lunch the next day, Mr Smart said, 'There, Nat, aren't you glad you went to church?'

Mrs Smart had been right. The drama group did perform.

Their story this time was the Parable of the Lost Sheep. In the story, Jesus told how a shepherd went to count his sheep and discovered that one of them was missing. So off the shepherd went to hunt high and low until he found the one that was lost. Which meant that this time, the drama group weren't looking for seeds or weeds. This time, they wanted volunteers to pretend to be sheep. And they wanted one sheep in particular to get lost.

Nat put up his hand. Sparky put up her hand too. Nat was picked to be the sheep who got lost because he was a visitor.

He was good too. Very good. **He got very, *very* lost.**

He got *so* lost in fact that, in the end, the shepherd hunting for him had to give up because it was time for Junior Church to go out to their groups. If they didn't go out on time, then everything else would run behind too. Especially the coffee and juice and biscuits at the end of the service. And, let's face it, *no one* wanted that.

'So, Nat,' said Mr Smart, 'how exactly did you find your way into the bell tower?'

Nat shrugged his shoulders. 'I saw the sign that said *No entry*.'

Mr Smart's eyebrows went up. 'I see,' he said. 'You saw a sign that said *No entry*, so you thought it would be a perfect place to, in fact, enter.'

Nat nodded. 'Best hiding place in the church. If there's a *No entry* sign up, you wouldn't expect someone to have gone in there to hide. Would you?'

'No,' agreed Mr Smart. 'Probably not.'

Sparky was impressed. She'd been impressed ever since Nat had been discovered in the bell tower at the end of the morning service.

'It was a really cool hiding place,' she said.

'Erm, yes,' said Mrs Smart. 'The thing is though, Nat, when no one came to find you – after *quite* a while – didn't you think that there might be a problem?'

'No,' said Nat. 'I just thought it was a really cool hiding place.'

'Right,' said Mrs Smart. 'Good.'

'Yes,' said Mr Smart. 'Good. And ten out of ten for inventiveness in the hiding-place-finding department, obviously. But perhaps, another time, if you see a *No entry* sign, you might want to think twice about... entering.'

'In church?' asked Nat.

'Anywhere,' said Mr Smart.

'Absolutely anywhere,' said Mrs Smart. '*No entry* signs

are there for a reason, Nathaniel. You should take notice of them.'

Mr Smart began to spoon vegetables onto his plate. He ate a lot of vegetables. 'Vegetables are at the heart of a healthy diet,' he would say. Quite often.

'The thing is, though, Nat,' said Stanley, 'your hiding place ruined the story.'

'Did it?' asked Nat.

'Jesus told the story of the lost sheep because He wanted people to know that God is like the shepherd. The shepherd cared about the lost sheep so much that he didn't stop searching for it until he found it,' said Stanley. 'And God cares about people so much that He never stops looking for us either, because He wants every single one of us to be His friends.'

Nat looked at him. 'So, what's the problem?'

Stanley raised his eyes. 'The problem is,' he said, 'you made the shepherd give up because he couldn't find you! And that's not the point of the story – because **God never gives up!**'

There was silence for a moment.

'That's true actually, Nat,' said Sparky. 'But it doesn't change the fact that it was a really cool hiding place.'

Sissy banged her spoon on the table. 'Coo iking case,' she said.

'Right,' said Mr Smart, 'who else is for vegetables?'

Archie made a face. 'Not me, thanks. I don't like them.'

'Come on, Archie,' said Mr Smart, 'pass me your plate.'

'But I don't like them,' Archie said.

'Did you know,' said Mr Smart, 'that the more you do something, the more you get used to it?'

'You said that last time we were here,' said Archie.

'And it obviously doesn't apply to homework,' said Nat. 'Because I've been getting homework from school for ages and I still haven't got used to it.'

Mr Smart reached over and picked up Archie's plate. 'Just a few, eh?'

He served out several slices of carrot and a small heap of cabbage. 'Because I'll tell you what, Archie, vegetables,' he said, 'are at the heart of a healthy diet.'

'Elfy dit,' said Sissy.

Sunday evening in termtime was never a good time for anything to go wrong. When Mrs Smart had school on a Monday morning, everything on a Sunday night needed to go as smoothly as possible. Otherwise, there might well be shouting.

This Sunday evening wasn't in termtime, it was the holidays. So, thought Sparky, *things could actually have been a lot worse*.

You may remember that Stanley was very interested in how things worked. Well, it has to be said, Sparky, was also very good at knowing when they were about to *stop* working.

When Mrs Smart was blow-drying her hair one morning, Sparky had been the one to notice the odd, whizzy noise the dryer was making, just before it went 'phut' and gave up.

'I think your hair dryer's about to go "phut",' Sparky had said – just as it did.

Another time, when Mr Smart was vacuuming the hall

carpet, it was Sparky who smelled the rather disgusting stink of burning rubber, right before the vacuum cleaner died, with a loud **BANG**.

'Dad, I think the vacuum's about to go "BANG",' Sparky had said – just as her dad had exploded with the biggest sneeze she'd ever heard in her life. It almost drowned out the 'BANG' from the vacuum cleaner.

'Dad, couldn't you smell that disgusting burning rubber smell?' Sparky had asked.

'Can't smell a thing,' mumbled Mr Smart. 'I've got the worst cold I've ever had in my life.'

On this particular Sunday evening, Sissy was being difficult. She didn't want to go to bed.

The Smarts' house had only three bedrooms, not the four that Mrs Smart dreamed of. So Sissy had to share a bedroom with Sparky.

Sparky had never been completely happy with this arrangement. Especially now that Sissy was no longer in a cot, but had her own little bed. Not only did this mean that Sparky had far less space in her bedroom; it also meant that, without the bars of the cot, Sissy now had complete freedom. She could get out of bed whenever she wanted. Which she did. Often.

On the evenings when Sissy was feeling difficult, Sparky sometimes went up later at her own bedtime, to find that she couldn't actually go to bed. This was because Sissy had done what Mrs Smart called a 'bed swapsy', and was already in it.

Mrs Smart looked tired when she came downstairs that Sunday evening. Still, on her fifth go at getting little Sissy to stay in bed, she had at last won the battle.

Or so she thought.

Mrs Smart headed for the kitchen, where she planned to make an extra-large pot of tea. She had an extra-large teapot for just those trying-sorts-of-evenings, when two mugs were never enough.

But before she even got there, Sissy was once more at the top of the stairs. She peeped over the stair gate.

'Up, Mummy.'

Mrs Smart took a deep breath. 'Fine,' she sighed.

'Can I do anything?' asked Stanley. He hadn't spotted an eye twitch yet but he knew it wouldn't be long.

'Oh, yes, thank you, Stanley,' said Mrs Smart. 'How kind of you. Can you put the washing on, please? It's all out ready. Ooh, and get the boys to come and watch. I'm pretty sure they haven't a clue how to work a washing machine.'

'Seriously?' said Stanley. 'You seriously want me to show Nat and Archie how to put on washing? They're ten years old.'

'Absolutely. You're never too young to learn how to do the washing. Come on then, Missy Sissy,' she said as she plodded back up the stairs. 'Now, what does "stay in bed" mean, eh? Believe it or not it means you *stay in bed*.'

Twenty minutes later, Sissy was at long last asleep upstairs while the Smarts and the crinkly cousins were playing *Cluedo* in the lounge.

Suddenly, Sparky stood up.

'Whatever's the matter, Sparky?' said Mrs Smart. 'You nearly knocked Professor Plum into my cup of tea.'

'Did you hear that?' said Sparky.

'Hear what?' said Mr Smart.

'That!' said Sparky. 'That sort of... gurgling noise.'

'Didn't hear a thing,' said Mr Smart. 'Come on, whose go is it?'

'No, ssshh!' hissed Sparky. She put a finger to her lips.

'I might have heard something,' said Nat. 'Then again, I might not.'

Sparky took in a sharp breath. 'There it is... a gurgle. You must have heard it that time.'

No one else had heard it. Except for Nat, who, again, might have heard it... or might not.

There were three possibilities here, Sparky thought. Either she was imagining the gurgle – which wasn't very likely. She wasn't the sort of girl to imagine things like a gurgle.

Or some strange alien creature had climbed in through the kitchen window and was, even now, gurgling its way through the chocolate biscuits that Mrs Smart kept hidden in a kitchen drawer (under the tea towels).

Or – and this was the worst, but most likely, possibility of all – the gurgles were coming from the washing machine.

'Mum?' said Sparky.

'Yes, Sparky,' said Mrs Smart.

'You know Auntie Bella said her washing machine was on the blink...'

'Yes, Sparky,' said Mrs Smart.

'Well,' said Sparky, searching for the right words so as not to cause alarm, 'wouldn't it be really... erm... *interesting,* if ours was on the blink too?'

'Sweetheart, don't be silly,' said Mr Smart. 'Just because Auntie Bella's washing machine is "on the blink", as you put it, that doesn't mean there's anything wrong with ours.'

'Are you sure about that?' said Sparky. 'Because for a washing machine that's not on the blink, it's making an awful lot of gurgles...'

This time, the gurgles sounded loud and clear. Everyone heard them – Smarts and crinkly cousins (let's call them the CCs for short) alike.

Mrs Smart shot up. The move was so sudden that, this time, Professor Plum did end up in her cup of tea. Plop.

'Oh, no!' shrieked Mrs Smart. 'The washing machine's on the blink!'

She rushed out to the kitchen. The rest of the Smarts and the two CCs rushed after her.

And – dear, oh, dear – Sparky was right again. This time, it was indeed the washing machine that was about to stop working.

At least, it certainly wasn't working properly. The clothes that Stanley had stuffed in 20 minutes before were still slopping round and round behind the glass door. But the water, which normally stayed inside the machine, was now running out surprisingly quickly from underneath. It had already made quite a large pool on the kitchen floor.

'Quick!' said Mr Smart. '**Turn it off! Turn it off!**'

Mrs Smart had already charged – well, splashed – across the kitchen and thumped the 'off' button. The machine went quiet. The clothes stopped slopping. But the water, unfortunately, continued to run out.

It kept running out until all the water that had been inside the machine was now outside the machine.

'All hands to the pumps!' yelled Mr Smart.

'**Sssh!**' hissed Mrs Smart. '*Please* don't wake Sissy. It's already taken me half the evening to get her to go to sleep.'

'What pumps?' said Archie. 'I can't see any pumps.'

'It's a thing they say on ships,' said Sparky, 'when there's water coming in. Sailors have to man the pumps to pump it out again.'

'Well, they wouldn't anymore,' said Stanley.

'Why not?' asked Sparky.

'Because it's not the olden days, is it? Everything's done by machine now.'

'That's right,' said Mr Smart. 'Nowadays if someone says, "All hands to the pumps", it means they need to get on and do something urgently.'

And speaking of urgency, the water had just reached Nat's toes. 'My socks are getting wet,' he said.

'Glad I'm not wearing any,' said Sparky, whose bare feet were already soaked.

'Well, don't just stand there yacking, everybody!' Mrs Smart threw her hands in the air. 'Grab something and help me mop!'

Half an hour or so later, the kitchen floor was just about back to normal.

Mrs Smart flopped down on the sofa in the lounge. 'Thank goodness,' she said, 'that we're a family with many towels.'

At bedtime, Archie asked, 'What are we doing tomorrow?'

'Have a guess,' said Sparky. 'Waiting around for the washing machine repair man...'

* * * *

On Monday, Mr Smart arrived home from work in the late afternoon to find the whole house in a bad mood.

It was half past five. The Smarts and the CCs had stayed in all day, waiting for the washing machine repair man.

The washing machine repair man had rung once. 'I should be there in the next two hours,' he'd said.

When he didn't arrive, Mrs Smart had rung him once. 'I should be there in the next two hours,' he'd said again.

So far, there was still no sign of him.

'The thing is, though,' said Sparky, 'we don't know where he's coming from because we didn't ask. I mean, he could be coming from as far away as Scotland.'

'Or the moon,' Stanley grunted. He looked miserable.

'Well, this is daft,' said Mr Smart. He didn't look too happy either. 'I need to throw my kit straight in the wash. I've been sweating buckets today.'

Mr Smart often arrived home quite sweaty. He was a personal trainer. That meant he helped people who weren't very fit to get fitter. He would take them running. He would work with them in the gym. Sometimes he even taught grown-ups how to swim. (Yes, there are actually a few grown-up people who have never learned to swim.)

Having a dad who was a personal trainer was, in some ways, quite fun. (As long as you remembered not to hug him when he came home from a running day. Sparky had discovered long ago that hugging a sweaty dad was icky in every way.) Mr Smart was always ready to kick a ball about with Sparky or Stanley or any of their friends.

He was always happy to play rounders down at the park, or surprise his children with unusual (some might say dangerous) obstacle courses he'd devised.

In other ways, Sparky always thought, having a dad who was a personal trainer wasn't fun at all. Often, Mr Smart was keen to do all those things when all Stanley and Sparky wanted to do was play video games or watch TV. And he would keep on and on until he got his own way. As for the fathers' race on school sports day, Mr Smart always got rather over-excited. So much so that, for the rest of the afternoon, Sparky and Stanley were forced to pretend that he wasn't their dad at all.

Today had been a running day. After a running day, all Mr Smart wanted when he got home was to give himself and his clothes a jolly good wash.

'Yes, Dad,' Stanley responded, 'and while you've been sweating buckets, guess what we've been doing?'

Mr Smart sighed. 'I've no idea.'

'Nothing,' Stanley replied. **'Absolutely, totally and completely nothing at all.'**

Mr Smart raised an eyebrow. He looked at the gloomy line of faces in front of him. Stanley's, it has to be said, was the gloomiest of all.

'Absolly nuffting,' said Sissy.

Suddenly, Mr Smart seemed to forget about his sweatiness. He smiled at Mrs Smart. 'Bad day?' he asked.

'Let me see,' said Mrs Smart, 'how shall I answer that?'

'Actually,' said Sparky, 'although we did absolutely, totally and completely nothing at all, quite a lot happened.'

'Did it?' said Mr Smart. There was a hint of anxiety in

his voice.

'Oh, yes,' said Sparky. 'I decided to write it all down in my diary.'

'I didn't know you kept a diary,' said Stanley.

'I don't,' said Sparky. 'Well, not usually. But I did today because we were doing absolutely, totally and completely nothing at all.'

Sparky's diary went like this...

SPARKY'S DIARY FOR MONDAY

When nothing happens, this is what happens:

1. Wanted to play *Monopoly*, but couldn't find it.
2. Sissy found Mum's lipstick, and drew all over the toilet with it.
3. The end fell off the lipstick. Nat trod in it by mistake and made lipsticky splodges on the landing carpet.
4. Archie decided to make his own lunch while Mum was upstairs cleaning up the lipstick. He put two crumpets in the toaster but only one popped up. The other one got stuck and caught fire.
5. We discovered that the smoke alarm works really well. It kept going off for at least the next hour.
6. We found *Monopoly*, but Nat didn't want to play anymore. He said all the pipping from the smoke alarm had given him a headache. So had all the smoke.

7. Stanley said he was going to his room to practise being a weather person. Nat said he couldn't, as he had to lie down in there because of his headache.

8. Mum ran out of tea bags.

9. Auntie Bella rang to say her life was VERY stressful at the moment and could Nat and Archie stay till Sunday. (Mum said no.)

10. Sissy bit me.

'Dad?' said Sparky.

'Yes, Sparky,' said Mr Smart.

'Do you know what I think God would want you to do in this situation?'

'Tell me,' said Mr Smart.

'I think He'd want you to cook dinner so Mum can have a rest.'

'Yes,' said Mr Smart. 'I think you're probably right.'

Dad went upstairs to have a quick shower. Then he did cook dinner.

He put it all out on the table in the kitchen and everyone sat down.

That's when the front doorbell rang.

It was the washing machine repair man.

On Tuesday morning at breakfast, Mrs Smart said, 'Today is going to be a better day. I can feel it in my bones.'

Stanley had unexpectedly been invited to a friend's house for the day. This was a good thing for two reasons.

Number one – it meant that Stanley could escape from the CCs for a few hours.

Number two – there was now enough room in the car for the other four children.

'Shall we make a plan?' asked Sparky.

'I've already got one,' Mrs Smart replied. And she winked. It was definitely a wink and not an eye twitch.

Hmm, thought Sparky. *Mum never winks.* ***This must be the best plan ever!***

It was. A picnic was packed in two carrier bags, then loaded into the car. The wellies were put in too – just in case.

Then, once everyone was strapped into their seats, Mrs Smart made her announcement.

'We're going to the castle,' she said.

Sparky's eyes opened very wide. 'The castle?' she repeated. 'Really? Creepy Castle? Really and truly?'

Creepy Castle (not its real name, but that's what Sparky called it) was about an hour and a half away by car. Sparky and Stanley had only ever been there once, on a day out with their dad.

Sparky had wanted to move in. She had even picked her bedroom. It would have been a bit cold and draughty, as Creepy Castle didn't have a roof and was mostly a ruin. But Sparky had insisted she would be fine with a hot water bottle.

'Why is it a ruin?' she had asked.

'If I was 750 years old,' Mr Smart had answered, 'I think I might be a bit of a ruin too.'

The Smarts and the CCs piled into the car.

'Ready?' asked Mrs Smart.

'Ready!' everyone replied.

Well, everyone except Sissy who said, 'Eggy!'

This made Nat and Archie laugh, so she kept on saying it. **'Eggy, eggy, eggy!'**

Sissy was still saying it long after Nat and Archie had stopped laughing.

And why had they stopped laughing? Because the car wouldn't start.

The car wouldn't start over... and over... and over again. Until Mrs Smart, with three by-now-very-grumpy-passengers and a fourth one shouting 'Eggy!', were forced to climb out again.

They all stomped into the house where Mrs Smart rang the breakdown people.

'Someone will be with you in the next two hours,' said a voice on the other end of the phone.

Oh, really, thought Mrs Smart. *And where have I heard that before?*

* * * *

On Wednesday morning, Archie found Sparky curled up in a corner of the lounge with her eyes closed.

'Are you praying?' Archie asked.

Sparky opened her eyes to find herself almost nose to nose with Archie.

'Pardon?' Sparky said.

'Are you praying?' asked Archie again.

'No,' said Sparky. 'Why?'

'Because you're sitting there with your eyes closed and I know you do praying.'

'You don't have to close your eyes to pray,' said Sparky. 'You don't have to sit down either.'

'Oh,' said Archie.

'Lots of times I talk to God with my eyes wide open,' Sparky added. 'Especially if I'm walking about. Otherwise I'd crash into things.'

Archie's face frowned. 'You talk to God when you're walking about?' he said.

'Walking about, standing still, in the car, doing one of Dad's *hideous* obstacle courses,' said Sparky. 'Pretty much anywhere really. Just like you'd do with a friend.'

'Oh,' said Archie again.

'Out loud, in my head,' said Sparky. 'You should try it. We talk, God listens. That's the way it is.'

If Archie was about to say 'Oh' for the third time, he didn't get the chance.

'We're going for a walk, apparently.' Stanley stood in the doorway.

Archie's face frowned again. 'I thought the car was fixed.'

'It Is,' said Stanley. 'But *I'm* here today, so we won't all fit in.'

Mrs Smart appeared. 'Let's all go for a lovely walk,' she said. 'After yesterday, what we need is a good dose of fresh air.'

'After yesterday *and* the day before,' said Sparky.

'Well, yes,' agreed Mrs Smart. 'Cars and washing machines, eh? Who'd have them?'

'By the way,' said Archie to Sparky. 'If you weren't praying, why were you sitting on the floor with your eyes closed?'

Sparky shrugged. 'I was imagining what it would be like to be a spider,' she said, and she went to find her shoes.

'Everyone ready?' called Mrs Smart ten minutes later.

'Yeah...' No one was quite as excited as they had been about yesterday's Creepy Castle announcement, but still. Even a walk was better than sitting around doing nothing for a third day in a row.

'Then off we go,' said Mrs Smart.

Mrs Smart wasn't sure what happened next. To be honest, no one was. One minute she was pushing Sissy in her pushchair out through the front doorway and the next, Stanley seemed to have somehow tripped over his own feet. As he tried to avoid crash-landing on the pushchair, he lost his balance completely and fell off the front step. He twisted and landed hard on his right foot, and his ankle promptly gave way.

'Ow!' Stanley howled. **'OOOWW!'**

'What is it, Stanley?' said Mrs Smart. 'What have you done?'

'I've broken it!' Stanley wailed. 'I think I've broken my ankle!' He sat down on the ground with a thud.

Sparky crouched beside him. 'I think you're right,' she said, peering at the injured limb. 'That's definitely a broken ankle. It's the most broken ankle I think I've ever seen.'

'Oh, don't be so silly,' said Mrs Smart. 'No one breaks their ankle falling off a little step like that.'

She parked the pushchair safely and bent down to look too.

Stanley's ankle appeared normal. It wasn't bent the wrong way. Nothing was sticking out. It wasn't even the tiniest bit swollen.

'Stanley, your ankle's fine, darling,' she said, 'and we're going for a walk.'

Stanley started to wail again. 'I can't go for a walk now. It hurts. **It *really* hurts!** Anyway, how do you know it's not broken? It might be. Just because it looks all right to you doesn't mean it is!'

'Stanley, please get up,' said Mrs Smart. 'It's Wednesday already and so far we've done nothing all week.'

'Yeah, and it's been really boring,' moaned Nat.

Mrs Smart sighed. 'Come on, up you get so we can all go for a walk.'

'*I* know!' said Sparky. Her eyes were bright with an idea. 'Why doesn't Sissy walk? Then we can all push Stanley in the pushchair?'

'Sabrina,' said Mrs Smart, 'when was the last time you saw a 13-year-old boy in a toddler's pushchair? Now, Stanley, will you *please get up*!'

Stanley did get up. Eventually. But as for walking, the furthest the Smarts and the CCs managed to go was up the front step and back into the house.

☆ ☆ ☆ ☆

On Thursday morning, Mr Smart woke up with a toothache. It was bad too – at least, that's what Mr Smart said.

'You do look a bit pale, Dad,' said Sparky. Then, 'No,' she said, 'not pale. More sort of yellowy with a bit of...' She thought for a moment. 'Yellowy with a bit of purple, I reckon.'

'Thanks, Sparky,' said Mr Smart.

'No worries,' said Sparky.

Mr Smart's sudden toothache was unfortunate,

because he'd taken the day off to join in a family trip to the beach. It was the CCs' last day with the Smarts. Mr Smart was going to drive one car and take Sparky, Nat and Archie. Mrs Smart was going to drive the other car, and take Stanley and Sissy. (Stanley's ankle, by the way, was very much not broken. 'It *could* have been, though,' he insisted.)

Today was going to be fun. Huge fun. Let's face it, when you've been cooped up inside a house doing nothing for three days, how could it be anything else?

The big question was, how was Mr Smart going to drive a car packed with three children and a picnic all the way to the beach, when he had such a poorly tooth?

Well, the answer was – he couldn't. He did manage to drive himself to the dentist later that day to find that his tooth had cracked in a big way and needed fixing. And when he came home, he couldn't speak properly. He'd had one of those injections that make your face go numb, so he could hardly move his mouth.

Mrs Smart made him some soup for dinner. Mr Smart might have smiled if his mouth had worked. But he looked grateful, if still yellow and a bit purple, and took a slurp.

'Funk oo,' he said, with soup trickling down his chin.

* * * *

Auntie Bella arrived unexpectedly at ten o'clock the next morning. It was unexpected because she was on time. Auntie Bella was never on time.

'Why aren't you ready?' Auntie Bella asked.

Nat and Archie had had breakfast and done most of

their packing, but they were still in their pyjamas.

'Go and get dressed. Quickly!'

Auntie Bella sighed as if she'd already been waiting for at least an hour.

'So,' said Mrs Smart, 'did you enjoy your bit of peace and quiet?'

'Peace and quiet?' said Auntie Bella. 'Have you any idea how busy I've been this week? I haven't stopped. It's been one thing after another, and of course nothing ever goes to plan. I was supposed to be having my hair done on Wednesday – not a hope. And as for having time to go food shopping, ha! I've eaten nothing but takeaways all week long.'

'You've still got work coming out of your eyeballs, then?' inquired Sparky.

'Eyeballs, ears, and armpits, more than likely!' said Auntie Bella.

Armpits?! Eew... thought Sparky. She decided not to picture that one.

Nat and Archie reappeared, dressed and ready to go.

'Will you stop for a cup of tea?' asked Mrs Smart.

'Gosh, no!' Auntie Bella almost laughed. 'People like me rarely have time to stop for anything. No, must dash. Thank you SO much for having the boys, Stell. I'm sure they've had the most marvellous time. Go on, boys, thank Auntie Stella for the marvellous time you've had.'

'Erm...' mumbled Nat. 'Thanks for the... erm... well, thanks.'

'Me too,' said Archie. 'It's been... yeah.'

Mrs Smart didn't have the chance to give the crinkly cousins a goodbye hug. Auntie Bella was already dragging the one-wheel-short suitcase towards the car.

'Come on then, boys!' she called. 'Tell me all about it on the way home.'

Sissy stood on the doorstep and flapped a hand up and down in a sort of wave. Mrs Smart and Sparky waved too. Stanley didn't wave. He stuck his hands in his pockets and breathed a huge sigh of relief.

'Right,' said Mrs Smart. She scooped little Sissy, whose hand was still flapping up and down, into her arms. 'I think the best thing we can all do is put this week very firmly behind us – and never mention it again.'

'Sounds good to me,' said Stanley.

'Me too,' agreed Sparky.

'And you know what sounds good to me?' said Mrs Smart. 'A nice cup of tea.'

The mysterious case of the vanishing slippers

Grandad Bagg was the best grandad in the whole world.

Sparky had told him this often. 'And when you think, Grandad,' she would add, 'how many grandads there must be in the whole entire world, and you're the best one of all – that must make you really, *really* special.'

Grandad Bagg was Mrs Smart's dad. Mrs Smart always said that he was the best dad as well as the best grandad. And when Mrs Smart's mum had died ten years ago, Grandad had decided to move house to be closer to his family.

He couldn't have moved much closer to the Smarts. He now lived in the next street. That might be too close for some grandads, especially those who want a quiet life. But Grandad Bagg had never lived a quiet life before and he had no intention of starting now. Which was just as well, given all the child-minding he was asked to do.

One of the most interesting things about Grandad Bagg was all the different jobs he'd had. He'd been a mechanic and a bus driver. He'd almost become a train driver, but had changed his mind at the last moment. He'd run his own carpet and window-cleaning business. He'd knocked on doors selling household cleaning products. He'd even been the driver for 'quite an important person', although he would never say who.

But Grandad's favourite job by far was being a ferryman. Sparky and Stanley loved it when Grandad Bagg talked about his ferryman days. From morning to night, he would steer a small passenger ferry back and forth across the river near where he used to live, so that people could get from one side to the other.

While Mrs Smart sometimes had a twitch in her eye, Grandad Bagg had a twinkle in his that never went away.

He'd twinkled more than ever the day he had said to Sparky and Stanley, 'Of course, I might NOT have been a mechanic, or a bus driver, or nearly a train driver. I might NOT have run a carpet and window-cleaning business or knocked on doors selling household cleaning products, or been the driver for "quite an important person". I might not even,' he had added, '*ever* have been a ferryman.'

'Why not?' Sparky had asked.

'Because maybe – just maybe,' Grandad had said, leaning towards her and lowering his voice, 'I'm a secret agent and I work for a secret organisation doing secret things.'

Sparky's mouth had dropped open. 'Like what?' she had gasped.

'Ooh, I could never tell you that,' said Grandad. 'They're all far too secret...'

Sparky was five years old at the time. She'd never looked at Grandad Bagg in the same way again. Suddenly, he was no longer *just* the best grandad in the whole world. He was also 'Mr Mysterious'.

Grandad Bagg had been away on a coach trip the week the crinkly cousins came to stay. (Yes, *that* week. The one that's never to be mentioned again.) He'd been up to the Lake District in the north of England.

'There are lakes and mountains there like you've never seen,' he told Stanley and Sparky.

He was right. Stanley and Sparky had never seen them. But now they wanted to.

When Grandad Bagg had stepped through their

doorway after his holiday, one by one, all the Smarts gave him a hug. All except Stanley, that is, who was now far too grown up to hug anyone. Not even Mr Mysterious.

'Oh, Dad!' beamed Mrs Smart. 'How we've missed you!'

'It's true, we have,' said Sparky. 'And not just because we've had a *really* bad week that we're never going to mention again. We've missed your twinkles.'

'Tinkles,' said Sissy.

Grandad Bagg lifted Sissy up as she toddled towards him. He hadn't bothered to shave much while he was away. This meant there were a few rough and whiskery bits around his chin. Sissy started to tug at them. Her fingers were sticky because she'd just been eating (well, more like sucking, really) a jam tart.

'Ow! That's enough of that, Missy Sissy!' said Grandad, and he put her down. He rubbed his sore face – and wondered why it was sticky.

'So,' Grandad said, trying to ignore whatever the sticky stuff was on his fingers and on his chin, 'what was so bad about your week then?'

'I could tell you,' said Sparky, 'but like I say, we're never to mention it again.'

'But since we have mentioned it,' said Stanley, 'Nat and Archie came to stay.'

'**Aha!**' said Grandad. He nodded his head in a knowing sort of way. 'Say no more.'

Grandad was very fond of both his daughters (Stella and Bella). He was just as fond of all his grandchildren – the Smart ones and the crinkly ones. But he knew very well that when you put them all together, they didn't always mix.

‘Would you like a cup of tea, Dad?’ asked Mrs Smart. ‘And I’ve just made some jam tarts.’

‘Ooh, I love a jam tart – sounds perfect,’ said Grandad. ‘Do you mind if just nip and wash my hands first... and possibly my face?’

* * * *

If a day needed saving, it was very often Grandad who saved it. Provided, of course, he wasn’t on a coach trip in the Lake District.

Mrs Smart was in a panic.

She had woken up in a panic. Mr Smart had had to go to work and leave her in a panic. And Sissy hadn’t helped the situation by getting a sudden nosebleed. It wasn’t her fault, but it was a bit yucky to wake up to.

The main reason for Mrs Smart’s panic was that there were only five days left of the school holidays. Five days left in which to plan maths lessons. Maths lessons for the whole term.

FIVE DAYS!

Mrs Smart sat in bed, one hand pressed to her forehead. With the other hand, she held a tissue to Sissy’s nose.

‘How on earth am I supposed to do all my planning in only five days?’ she said. ‘Just the thought of it makes my head want to explode.’

‘Poor Mum,’ said Sparky, who had followed Sissy and her yucky nose into the bedroom. ‘Looks like you might have work coming out of your eyeballs, like Auntie Bella.’

Mrs Smart shook her head. ‘I’ve got much more work coming out of my eyeballs than Auntie Bella,’ she groaned. 'I don't know what I'm going to do. I need peace and quiet and space to do planning. And you're all here!'

'Sorry,' said Sparky.

'Oh, no, darling, I don't mean that! I love having you here.' Mrs Smart took the hand pressed to her forehead and ruffled Sparky's hair with it. It was already quite ruffled as Sparky had only just got out of bed. 'I wish I could just be here for you three all the time. But it's not like that. I have to earn money.' She sighed. 'And now the holidays are coming to an end, and I've *got* to get my planning done.'

Sparky nodded. 'I'll ring Grandad,' she said.

'Oh, yes, please, Sparky! Go and ring him now, would you? I know he's only just got back from holiday, but ask him if you and Sissy could go round for a couple of hours.'

'What about Stanley?'

'No, no, Stanley's fine,' said Mrs Smart. 'He's already told me he wants to spend the day in his room, practising to be a weather person. Apparently he's got a lot of weather to catch up on now that Nat and Archie aren't here.'

'Stanley's really quite odd, isn't he?' said Sparky.

Mrs Smart smiled. 'We're all pretty odd.'

'Plotty plod,' mumbled Sissy. It was hard to do anything but mumble with a tissue up your nose.

'And, Mum,' Sparky said, 'don't forget to ask God to help you with your planning. I'll ask Him too. He will help, you know. He helped me with the end of term spelling competition.'

'But you didn't win,' said Mrs Smart.

'Doesn't matter,' said Sparky. 'He still helped me.'

Mrs Smart looked as if she might burst into tears.

'Thank you, sweetheart, I won't forget to ask Him,' she said. 'We may be an odd family, but if God's happy with that, then so am I.'

❀ ❀ ❀ ❀

When people knocked on Grandad's door, he didn't always answer straightaway. This was sometimes because he was out.

At other times, it was because he spent a lot of time in his shed and in his greenhouse.

Even in the shed or the greenhouse, Grandad still might have heard the doorbell ring – if it wasn't for the singing.

Grandad's singing, that is.

Grandad Bagg loved to sing. He loved to sing songs from rather grand operas. Very loudly.

Sometimes the songs Grandad sang were in a different language. Whether he understood what the words meant or not was anyone's guess. But he sang them anyway.

It was a bit of a shock to start with, but Grandad's neighbours had got used to his singing over the years. Some even said they'd miss it if he stopped. And as Grandad Bagg was such a good neighbour in so many other ways, no one liked to complain.

The main reason Grandad Bagg sang in the greenhouse was because of his tomatoes. Every year, he grew the most beautiful tomatoes. Sparky always said that if her crinkly cousin Archie didn't like tomatoes, he would change his mind if he tried one of Grandad's. They were, quite simply, the best.

'It's because they know they're loved,' said Grandad. 'When I sing to my tomatoes, they know exactly how important they are to me. Everything needs a bit of love if it's going to grow strong and healthy.'

There was another reason Grandad liked to sing in the greenhouse (because, after all, tomatoes don't grow all year round). It was because it helped him imagine he was singing on stage at the Sydney Opera House in Australia.

Stanley had walked round to Grandad Bagg's with Sparky, who pushed Sissy in her pushchair. Stanley was helping by carrying a bag packed with some books, toys and DVDs, the rest of Mrs Smart's jam tarts, and a change of clothes in case of emergency. When Mrs Smart had wanted Grandad to look after Sparky and Sissy for a couple of hours, what she really meant was all day.

Stanley rang Grandad's doorbell.

They waited.

Stanley rang the doorbell again.

No one came.

'He must be in the greenhouse,' said Sparky.

'It's too early for tomatoes,' said Stanley, and he rang the doorbell once more.

This time, the front bedroom window swung open from the floor above them, and Grandad's head popped out.

'Won't be a minute,' Grandad called. 'I'm just looking for my socks.'

When Grandad at last opened the door, he was wearing his extra-special slippers, but he clearly had no socks on his feet.

Grandad's slippers were extra special because he'd bought them when he was on holiday in Canada the year before. They were very warm and very snuggly, and he loved them.

'I can't understand it,' he said. 'I went to the Lake District with a pile of socks. I wore a pile of socks while I was up there. Not all at the same time, obviously. But I seem to have come home with no socks.'

'What about the ones you were wearing yesterday?' asked Sparky.

'In the wash,' said Grandad.

'Oh. Well, didn't you leave any here?'

'Oh, no.' Grandad shook his head. 'Wherever I go, I always take all my socks. You can never be too careful when it comes to your feet. Remember that.'

Sparky was sure she would.

As soon as Stanley had gone home, Sissy began to unpack her toys in Grandad's lounge. Sissy's idea of unpacking was to pull the toys and books out of the bag, one after the other, and hurl them across the room. Grandad was hit on the knee by a flying cuddly tortoise called Richard. Sparky was hit in the stomach by one of Sissy's books. Fortunately, it had soft covers.

As another book flew through the air, it knocked into a vase. Grandad managed to catch the vase by doing a little sideways hop and a shuffle.

'Good job I used to do ballroom dancing,' he said.

'Grandad,' said Sparky, 'is there anything you *haven't* done?'

Grandad twinkled. 'No, Sparky,' he said, 'I'm not sure there is.'

'Wow,' admired Sparky, as a DVD whistled past her left ear.

'Missy Sissy!' said Grandad. '**Stop throwing things!** Now, who's for some ice cream, with a drizzle of honey from my china pot?'

One of the best things about being at Grandad's house without any other grown-ups, Sparky always thought, was that *anything* was possible. At home, no one would ever think to offer them ice cream with a drizzle of honey at half past nine in the morning. Especially not Mr Smart. 'If it's not healthy, it's not worth eating,' Mr Smart would say.

But here, in Grandad's house, a magical thing like eating ice cream with honey when you've only just had breakfast was normal. The most normal thing in the world.

The rest of the day was quite magical too. Grandad took Sparky and Sissy on a 'Great Sock Hunt'. There weren't many places to look for Grandad's missing socks. They could only really be in his suitcase or his rucksack. And as he'd already emptied these and his socks weren't in either, that was the end of it. But calling it a 'Great Sock Hunt' made it sound so much more interesting. It also seemed to help Grandad realise that it wasn't just his socks that were missing. He'd lost a whole bag of dirty washing.

They played games together and went for a walk to the stream. Grandad read stories and showed Sparky and Sissy lots of his holiday photos from the Lake District.

'If you look at them hard enough,' Grandad said, 'perhaps you'll spot my washing.'

They didn't.

In the middle of the afternoon, Sissy had a short nap. When she woke up, she wanted to watch *Peppa Pig*, so Grandad put it on for her.

'You're always so kind to us, Grandad,' said Sparky. 'And silly and funny.' She put her arms round him and squeezed. 'And you've got a lovely squidgy tummy.'

'Oi!' said Grandad. 'Cheeky!'

'But it suits you perfectly,' said Sparky. 'I think God must be a bit like you.'

'Why?' said Grandad. 'Has God got a squidgy tummy too?'

'Maybe,' said Sparky. 'But Mum says God's always the same. He's never in a bad mood and He's always kind.

And that's like you. I mean, you've lost all your socks and most of your dirty washing, and you're not cross or anything.'

'Well,' said Grandad, 'I'll let you into a secret. I hate doing washing. So if I've lost it, I can't do it, can I?'

Then, 'Come out to the greenhouse for a minute, Sparky,' he said. 'You can help me plant some tomato seeds. We'll be right back, Sissy,' he added. 'We're only in the garden.'

Grandad left his extra-special slippers from Canada by the back door and tucked his bare feet into his wellies.

'**Oooh!**' he shivered. '**They're a bit chilly.**'

Sparky followed him out to the greenhouse.

She planted ten tomato seeds in ten different small pots. Grandad put Sparky's pots in a special place in the greenhouse so that she'd know which ones were hers. Then she'd be able to keep an eye on how her very own tomato plants were getting on.

A short while later, Sparky went back indoors. Grandad said he'd be there in a moment.

Sparky didn't notice that Grandad's slippers were no longer by the back door. Not at first.

No, the first thing she noticed was that Sissy wasn't on the sofa watching *Peppa Pig*. Instead, Sparky found her sitting under the kitchen table. Sissy had taken Grandad's china honey pot from on top of the table and was now spooning honey into her mouth.

But not just into her mouth.

She had also found Grandad's slippers and was spooning honey into those too.

Sparky gasped. 'Sissy!'

The slippers had dribbles of honey running down their sides. On the insides, pools of golden stickiness soaked the fluffy linings and oozed towards the toes.

'**What have you done?** Those are Grandad's extra-special, warm and snuggly slippers from Canada!' Sparky cried. 'And he's already lost his socks. Now he won't be able to wear his snuggly slippers either!'

Sissy grinned. 'Uggy ippers,' she said.

Sometimes, Sparky couldn't help wondering why her parents had wanted another baby.

Clearly some quick thinking was called for. Some very quick thinking, because any minute now, Grandad would be back from the greenhouse.

Grandad was so kind and squidgy, and Sparky couldn't bear the thought of him seeing his beautiful slippers, all the way from Canada, horrible and sticky and covered in honey. Grandad loved his slippers. He'd be so upset. Especially seeing as he now didn't have any socks.

So Sparky's quick-thinking brain sprang into action.

'Right,' she said, 'we can't possibly let Grandad see

what you've done. And anyway, he can't put his feet in those. They might get stuck. Forever. He might never get them out again! He might have to walk around in his slippers and go to bed in his slippers for the rest of his life – whether he wants to or not!'

Sparky thought for a moment.

'*I* know!' Her eyes lit up the way they always did when she had a brilliant idea. 'I'll take them home and wash them, and bring them back tomorrow. He'll never know. He'll just think he's put them somewhere, but can't remember where.'

Sparky grabbed the sticky, drippy slippers. She also grabbed a plastic carrier bag from Grandad Bagg's bag drawer (thank goodness she knew where his bag drawer was!), and shoved the slippers into it. Then she put the whole lot into the bag they'd brought from home. She threw a few books in there too, to hide it.

There wasn't, however, much that Sparky could do about Sissy. Even washing her hands wouldn't help. She was so covered in honey, only a bath would do.

When Grandad came in from the garden, Sparky said, 'I'm so sorry, Grandad, but Sissy's been eating honey from your china honey pot.'

Grandad had now taken off his boots. He stood by the back door in his bare feet, looking down.

'Now that's odd,' he said. 'I'm sure I left my slippers here.'

'Erm... did you?' said Sparky. 'I can't see them.'

'Neither can I,' said Grandad. 'Which is why it's odd because I know this is where I left them.'

'When you say "slippers",' said Sparky, 'which slippers was it exactly?'

‘The slippers I’ve been wearing nearly all day,’ said Grandad. ‘The slippers I took off when we went down to the greenhouse, and left by the back door.’

‘But did you, though?’ said Sparky. Her quick-thinking brain was once again doing some quick thinking. ‘I mean, you *thought* you’d brought your socks home from the Lake District, didn’t you? But you haven’t. Maybe you just *thought* you left your slippers by the back door, but actually you left them somewhere else.’

‘But didn’t you see me leave them by the back door?’

‘Erm…’ said Sparky. She put on her best thoughtful face. ‘Erm… let me think. I remember you putting your wellies on,’ she said, ‘but I don’t remember anything about your slippers.’

Grandad Bagg frowned. His bushy eyebrows almost met just above his nose. *A bit like Stanley’s caterpillars,* Sparky thought, although she’d never seen caterpillars as bushy as Grandad’s eyebrows.

‘Well, that’s just odd, that is,’ said Grandad. ‘I put them there, right there by the back door, and then I put my wellies on. And they’ve vanished. They’ve completely disappeared, as if they’ve walked off all by themselves.’

Grandad started to wander around the kitchen. He stooped a little and peered so that he could have a good look all over the floor.

He was so busy looking for his slippers that he didn’t notice the sticky honey patch that dribbled out from under the table – until he stepped in it. With one bare foot.

‘**What on earth…?**’ Grandad lifted up his one sticky foot to try to see underneath. Then he looked back down at the floor.

'It's honey,' said Sparky. 'From your china honey pot. Sissy found it while we were in the garden. I did say but you didn't hear because of your vanishing slippers.'

That's when Grandad noticed the sticky blob under the kitchen table. The sticky blob that was Sissy, with honey on her fingers and all over her face, honey down her jumper and drizzled on her skirt, and honey in her hair.

'Oh, dear,' said Grandad. He put his hands on his hips. 'Well, what a sticky, icky mess, eh, Missy Sissy?'

'Sticky-kicky,' said Sissy.

Sparky thought the best thing now was to be very positive. 'Good job Mum always packs spare clothes,' she said, 'in case of emergency.'

When Grandad delivered Sparky and Sissy back home a short while later, Mrs Smart said, 'Thank you SO much, Dad. I don't know what I'd do without you.' And she gave him a kiss.

'Can we go to Grandad's again tomorrow?' asked Sparky quickly.

She had to go to Grandad's tomorrow so that she could return the slippers she would by then have washed and made un-sticky.

'Well...' said Mrs Smart.

'I just *love* being with Grandad.' Sparky put her arms around him and snuggled against his squidgy tummy to show she meant it. 'Please?'

'Well,' said Mrs Smart again, 'in some ways it would help. I've still got quite a lot of maths planning to do.'

Grandad put his arms around Sparky too. 'If it's all right with you, it's all right with me,' he said. 'They can help me hunt for my vanishing slippers.'

A short while after Grandad had gone home again, Sparky asked, 'Mum, can I have a bath, please?'

Mrs Smart raised her eyebrows. 'Why do you want a bath?' she asked. 'You only had a shower this morning. You don't even like baths.'

That was true. Sparky didn't like baths. How can you get properly clean, she always thought, if you're sitting in your own dirty water?

But the reason why Sparky suddenly *wanted* a bath was because she knew it was the best place to wash Grandad's sticky slippers. Of course, she couldn't tell Mum that.

'I don't like baths... usually,' she said. 'Only today, I'd really, *really* like to have one. So may I, please?'

Mrs Smart was a little confused. But as she was trying to print out her maths planning with only one free hand (Sissy had the other one and wouldn't let go), she didn't ask any more questions.

'Go and start to run it then,' Mrs Smart said. 'But don't get in until I've been up to check how hot the water is. The last thing we want is you burning yourself.'

So far so good, thought Sparky, and she bounded up the stairs.

Ten minutes later, Grandad's sticky slippers were in the bath with rather a lot of bubbles. Sparky wasn't in the bath with them. After all, how can you get properly clean if you're sitting in your own dirty water? In any case, no one wants to share a bath with a pair of slippers covered in honey.

No, Sparky leaned over the side of the bath and slopped the slippers about. She scrunched them up in the

bubbles and let them go – and scrunched them up and let them go again. She sloshed them from one end of the bath to the other quite a few times. Then she shook them about under the water.

'They *can't* be sticky anymore,' Sparky said to herself. And she lifted up a slipper to check.

She was right. All those bubbles and all that slopping and sloshing seemed to have done the trick. The stickiness was well and truly gone.

Hooray! thought Sparky. *What a good job I'm a quick thinker!*

It *was* a good job too. However, there was now another problem.

Grandad's slippers may not have been sticky anymore. But now, they were horribly soggy. All dripping and squelchy. They looked like two large, hairy guinea pigs that had got caught out in a rain storm. And it didn't matter how much Sparky tried to shake and twist and squeeze the water out. They still looked much more like sad, soggy guinea pigs than Grandad's slippers.

Oh, no! thought Sparky. *Now what am I going to do? How can I take Grandad's slippers back if they look like this? He's bound to notice. If he puts them on, he'll end up with soaking wet feet. And if he walks around in them, he'll leave soaking wet slipper marks all over his house.*

Sparky began to panic. She needed to do some more quick thinking. *I've got to think of something to help them to dry. But what can I do?* **WHAT CAN I DO?** *Oh, come on, think, Sparky, think! Quickly!*

Happily, Sparky's quick thinking didn't let her down.

She wrapped the slippers in her towel and put them in her bedroom. Then she emptied the bath and ran downstairs.

'Mum?' Sparky asked.

'Yes, Sparky,' said Mrs Smart. 'Did you enjoy your bath?'

'Pardon?' said Sparky. 'Oh, yes, it was lovely. May I have a hot water bottle, please? I've brought it down.'

Sparky held out her hot water bottle. It was inside a fluffy, orange, teddy bear cover.

'Sparky,' said Mrs Smart, '*why* do you want a hot water bottle?'

'Well, because I'm... cold,' said Sparky.

Sparky wasn't cold, of course. But her quick-thinking idea was that if her hot water bottle was filled with hot water, she could sit Grandad's slippers on top of it. With all that heat underneath them, Sparky was sure the slippers would dry in no time.

'Why are you cold?' asked Mrs Smart. All of a sudden, she looked worried. 'You've just had a hot bath. You shouldn't be cold. Aren't you feeling very well?'

Stanley walked in. 'Well keep away from me, then,' he said. '*I'm* not catching it.' And he turned around and walked out again.

'I'm feeling fine,' said Sparky, in a reassuring voice. 'Very well, actually. Can I have the hot water bottle now?'

'Come here a minute,' said Mrs Smart.

Sparky sighed, but shuffled towards her. Mrs Smart put out her hand to touch Sparky's forehead.

'Well, you don't feel hot so I don't think you've got a high temperature,' she said. 'Because when you have a high temperature, that can make you feel cold.'

'I haven't got a high temperature,' said Sparky. 'I just want a hot water bottle.'

'Perhaps you should sit down quietly in the lounge for a bit. You've probably been on the go all day. I know what you're like when you go round to Grandad's.'

'I'm feeling fine,' said Sparky. 'I couldn't feel any better if I tried.' She hoped she sounded as normal as possible.

'And I don't need to sit down in the lounge and I haven't been on the go all day. All I want is a hot water bottle because I'm a bit cold – not a lot cold, just a bit cold. So please, please, PLEASE, can I just have one now?!'

Mrs Smart stared at her. There was a pause.

'Right,' she said. 'I'll put the kettle on.'

Having asked for a hot water bottle, Sparky now needed to show that she was cuddling it. But of course, she couldn't cuddle it because Grandad's soggy, guinea pig slippers needed it. So she had to stay in her bedroom, in bed, under her bedclothes. That way no one would guess that the hot water bottle wasn't being cuddled, but was actually *underneath* her bed doing a very important slipper-drying job.

This, of course, made Mrs Smart worry even more.

'What is it, Sparky?' she asked. There was lots of worry in her voice and quite a lot in her face too. 'Why are you in bed? Are you in pain? Does your tummy hurt? What about your head – have you got a headache? Do you feel snuffly at all?'

'I'm fine, Mum,' said Sparky.

'Well, I think I should ring the doctor,' said Mrs Smart.

'No!' said Sparky. 'You're the one who always says how busy doctors are and we should only bother them when it's "absolutely necessary".'

'Yes, but that's when you're pretending to have a tummy ache or a headache because you don't want to go to school. Besides,' said Mrs Smart, 'how do we know it's not absolutely necessary?'

'Well, keep away from me,' Stanley called from his bedroom. '*I'm* not catching it.'

Sparky sighed. She wondered if this conversation was going to go round and round in circles for a very long time.

It did.

When Mr Smart came home from work, the first thing Sparky heard Mrs Smart say to him was, **'I don't think Sparky's very well.'**

'What makes you say that?' asked Mr Smart.

'She's had a bath and she hates baths,' said Mrs Smart. 'Then she asked for a hot water bottle, and now she's gone to bed.'

'Odd,' said Mr Smart. 'Have you rung the doctor?'

'No,' said Mrs Smart. 'Sparky doesn't want me to.'

Mr Smart went upstairs and popped his head around Sparky's bedroom door. 'Everything all right, Sparky?' he said. 'Your mum thinks you're not feeling very well.'

'I'm feeling fine, Dad,' Sparky said. 'Honestly. See?' She held up the book she was reading. 'If I had a headache or a tummy ache, I'd be lying down. I'd probably be asleep. I definitely wouldn't feel like reading, would I?'

Mr Smart went back downstairs. 'She looks all right to me,' he said to Mrs Smart. 'She's not pale and she's not hot. I don't think there's anything to worry about.'

'I *am* all right,' Sparky called down the stairs. 'Nothing the matter with me at all!'

'Well, keep away from me,' shouted Stanley from the lounge. '*I'm* not catching it.'

When it was her proper bedtime, Sparky pulled Grandad's slippers on the hot water bottle out from under her bed. Her face fell.

The slippers were just as soggy as when she had first

put them under there. They didn't seem to be any drier at all. Not even the tiniest little bit.

Not only that, but the sogginess of the slippers had soaked into her fluffy, orange, teddy bear hot water bottle cover. So now it looked rather sad and damp too.

'**Oh, no!**' she groaned. 'These slippers are *never* going to dry. And when I ask Mum to put more hot water in my hot water bottle, she's going to wonder why the fluffy cover is all wet.'

Down in the kitchen, Sparky asked, 'Mum, please may I have some more hot water for my hot water bottle?'

'Of course you can, sweetheart,' said Mrs Smart. 'Oh. Where's the fluffy cover?'

Sparky had taken the damp fluffy cover off and stuffed it under her bed.

'Erm...' said Sparky. 'I've taken it off. Because I'm not always going to have a fluffy cover on my hot water bottle, am I? Not when I'm a grown-up. You and Dad have hot water bottles, but they don't have fluffy covers, do they?'

'Oh,' said Mrs Smart. 'Don't you like your fluffy hot water bottle cover anymore?'

'Oh, yes!' said Sparky. 'I *love* it. It's just so... well, fluffy. But the thing is, I've got to get used to not having it one day. You know, when I'm old like you and Dad. So I thought I may as well get used to it now. And Mum,' Sparky added, 'please could the water for the hot water bottle be extra, extra hot, because after all, it's got to last all night.'

Mrs Smart didn't put extra, extra hot water in Sparky's hot water bottle. Not only would Sparky have got burnt (especially now she didn't want to use the fluffy cover anymore), but the hot water bottle would also probably have burst.

'Night night, then,' whispered Mr Smart, when Sparky had climbed back into bed. Sparky's bedtimes were always whispered so as not to wake Sissy. Mr Smart kissed Sparky's forehead and turned to Mrs Smart.

'Her temperature's fine,' he whispered. 'She's not hot at all.'

'Well, that's good,' whispered Mrs Smart. 'But I think I'll ring Dad anyway. Probably better if you stay at home tomorrow, Sparky.'

Sparky's eyes widened in alarm. 'No!' Her 'no' came out quite loudly. Everyone glanced towards Sissy, but she was still sound asleep.

'No,' Sparky said again, in a whisper this time, 'I can't stay here tomorrow.'

Mrs Smart looked puzzled. 'Why not?'

'Because...' whispered Sparky, once again having to think quickly, '...because you've still got lots of work to do and I might be really annoying. I might interrupt you all the time. I might want more hot water bottles, or maybe even another bath. And I might have the TV on really, really loudly so you can't think straight. Because you *can't* think straight when the TV's on loud. You've said so – lots of times. You might get *nothing* done all day long. Besides, Grandad knows I'm going so we can't change it now.'

Sparky couldn't bear the thought of not giving Grandad back his slippers the next day. She had begun to think that the only thing her quick thinking had done was cause a great big muddle. It was a muddle she didn't want anymore and it wasn't even her fault. *She* wasn't the one who had filled Grandad's extra-special slippers from Canada with honey.

There was no sign of a twitch in Mrs Smart's eye, but both her eyes did narrow slightly. She looked at Sparky hard.

'Hmm...' she whispered. 'You're behaving very strangely, Sparky.'

Sparky looked back. *Phew!* she thought. *Mum called me Sparky, not Sabrina. That means I've* probably *got away with it.*

'So I'll go to Grandad's tomorrow, then,' whispered Sparky.

'We'll see how you are in the morning,' whispered Mrs Smart.

Fine, thought Sparky. *Because in the morning, I'll be FINE.*

'Well, keep away from me,' called Stanley from the bathroom. '*I'm* not catching it!'

'Sssh!' hissed Mr Smart.

☆ ☆ ☆ ☆

When Sparky woke up, it was still dark.

She hadn't meant to wake up in the middle of the night. But she was glad she had. It gave her time to check on Grandad's slippers before the morning.

Sparky pushed herself up on her elbows and peered towards Sissy. She couldn't see Sissy very well in the darkness, but she could hear her breathing. It was slow and deep and quite loud. When Sissy breathed like that, it meant she was asleep. Or that she had a very bad cold. Sissy didn't have a cold, so Sparky knew she was sleeping.

Gently, carefully, Sparky rolled over and began to lean out of bed. She stretched out an arm and felt around under the bed until her hand found the edge of her hot water bottle.

She pulled it out. It was just about cold.

She touched Grandad Bagg's slippers.

'Oh, no!'

It was only a whispered 'oh no'. Sparky couldn't afford to wake anyone up. Especially not Sissy, who would then wake up the whole house. When you hiss, 'Be very, *very* quiet and don't make a sound,' at a two-year-old, the chances are you won't get what you're hoping for.

In fact, it would probably have the very opposite effect from the one Sparky was after. She could imagine Sissy bursting into giggles – very loud giggles – and shouting, '**Bah! Bah, bah, bah, bah, BAH!**', also very loudly.

The more Sparky felt the slippers with her fingers, the more her heart sank. They were still soaking wet! Wet through and through. However many times she ran her fingers over them and patted them with the palm of her hand, they still felt far more like soggy guinea pigs than Grandad's extra-special slippers from Canada. There wasn't a dry bit of fluffiness to be found.

'Oh, no!' Sparky murmured again. For a minute, she thought she might cry.

Then, 'Pull yourself together,' she muttered to herself.

She'd heard Mrs Smart mutter this to herself many times. Especially if Mrs Smart had piles of homework to mark from her different maths classes, when all she really wanted was to sit down and do nothing. Even more so when there were so many piles of homework that she couldn't see the top of her desk.

Pull yourself together and think! Sparky drummed her fingers on her forehead. She needed an idea. A brilliant idea. How hard could it be? She wasn't called Sparky Smart for nothing – was she?

And then it happened. An idea hit her – smack bang in the middle of her forehead. It was as if her own caterpillar eyebrows had thrown themselves together, banged their heads, and shouted, 'OW!' at the same time.

It was all Sparky could do to stop herself from shouting, 'YES!'

And it was so simple, Sparky couldn't understand why she hadn't thought of it before.

What did her dad do with his personal trainer kit when he wanted it to dry in a hurry? (He never put his sports gear in the tumble dryer. He had done that once, and found that nothing fitted in quite the same way afterwards. In any case, if Sparky went down to the kitchen to use the tumble dryer in the middle of the night, questions would definitely be asked.)

No, the thing her dad did with his damp clothes was hang them in the airing cupboard!

The airing cupboard is a magical place found in some houses, and it's almost always warm, because of the tank of hot water inside it. When you turn on a hot tap in your home, it's very likely that your hot water comes from this tank. There are other ways to get hot water too. But we won't go into them here, because this is a storybook, not a science book.

YES! screamed Sparky in her head. *The airing cupboard! Why didn't I think of that before? If it's good enough for*

Dad's stinky sports kit, it's got to be good enough for Grandad's extra-special, soggy, guinea pig slippers!'

So, problem number one was solved. Probably.

However, problem number two was also rather tricky.

One of the difficulties with having to share a bedroom with your two-year-old sister was how easy it was to wake each other up.

In Sparky and Sissy's case, mostly it was Sissy who did the waking up.

Sissy would wake Sparky up by playing with her toys and making them talk to each other at full volume. Sissy had no idea how to play quietly.

Sissy would also wake Sparky up by sitting up in bed and calling, 'Mama!' at the top of her voice.

And, of course, Sissy loved to wake Sparky up by climbing onto her bed and bouncing up and down on top of her. When it came to waking her sister up quickly, Sissy often found this was the most effective method.

Now, on the flip side, once Sissy was finally asleep, she usually slept fairly deeply. But Sparky knew that if she was going to get out of bed, out of the room with Grandad's soggy slippers, all the way to the airing cupboard and back again, she would have to make no sound at all.

This would be a challenge.

And it wasn't just Sissy she had to worry about. Waking Stanley would be almost as bad. He would wake the rest of the house up too.

Come on, then, she said to herself silently. *Focus, and put your best foot forward.*

This is what Mr Smart always said to Sparky and

Stanley when they were about to start one of his death-defying obstacle courses. Come to think of it, Mr Smart's obstacle courses had probably been very good training for what Sparky was about to do.

Sparky didn't climb out of bed, she slithered. She could have got out normally. Getting out normally would have been just as quiet. But as she was on her way to do something that felt very daring and dangerous, slithering was more exciting.

Once on the floor, she picked up Grandad's soggy slippers, got to her feet, and tiptoed out of the room. She stopped once to listen. Sissy's breathing was still the slow, deep in-and-out of a sleeping two-year-old.

Phew, thought Sparky.

Sparky hadn't thought to look at the time. It was very dark, so it must be somewhere in the middle of the night. That was good enough. It meant that Grandad's slippers could hopefully stay in the airing cupboard for a good while.

Now all Sparky had to do was *get* to the airing cupboard. She wondered if God would be too busy to help her do that without waking anyone up. She decided to ask Him anyway. After all, she was trying to do a good thing, even though it had all got rather complicated.

Sparky tiptoed along the landing slowly. Very slowly.

At last, she reached the cupboard. She would have breathed a sigh of relief, if she hadn't been afraid that a sigh might wake someone up.

The airing cupboard was right outside Mr and Mrs Smart's bedroom. Sparky's next job was to push down the handle and open the door – silently.

Hmm, she thought. *How can one good idea have so many challenges?* She decided to ask God to help her with this one too.

Sparky felt that, to open the airing cupboard door, two hands would be better than one. That might give her more control. She put Grandad's slippers on the floor, reached out and grasped the handle with both hands. Then, very slowly and very gently, she began to push down.

As Sparky was about to discover, if a door handle has a squeak, it doesn't matter how many hands you use. Nor does it matter how slowly or how gently you move the handle. If it doesn't squeak going down, it will certainly squeak on the way back up.

Eeeek! went the handle – just to make the point.

If it had been daytime, it's probable that no one would have heard. In the daytime, the house was filled with so many other sounds, a squeaky door handle would go unnoticed.

But it was the middle of the night. The middle of a very still, very silent night. To Sparky, the squeak sounded like a small scream. And she wasn't the only one.

The light in Mr and Mrs Smart's bedroom flicked on almost at once. Sparky froze.

'Did you hear that?' Sparky heard Mrs Smart say.

'Hear what?' groaned Mr Smart.

'That noise.'

'What noise?'

'I don't know,' said Mrs Smart. 'It sounded like a small scream – didn't you hear it?'

'No, I was asleep,' mumbled Mr Smart. He sounded as if he would much rather still be asleep.

'So was I but I still heard it.' Mrs Smart sat up. 'Oh, my goodness, I think we might have a burglar.'

Mr Smart said nothing.

Mrs Smart turned and shook his shoulder. 'Wake up! I said there might be a burglar downstairs!'

'I'm sure we haven't got a burglar,' muttered Mr Smart. 'You were probably just dreaming. Go back to sleep.'

'How can I go back to sleep? I heard something. A scream.'

'Why would a burglar scream?' said Mr Smart. He sounded more awake now. He also sounded more annoyed. 'What would be the point of breaking into someone's house to burgle them, and then screaming?'

Suddenly, Mrs Smart had another thought. 'Sparky! It could be Sparky. I *told* you she wasn't feeling well.'

Mrs Smart threw back the covers and leapt out of bed. Fortunately, Sparky knew that she would. With a hand still pressed down on the squeaky handle, Sparky yanked open the airing cupboard door, grabbed Grandad's slippers, and tossed them inside. She just managed to slam the door shut again as Mrs Smart appeared in the bedroom doorway.

Mrs Smart was so shocked to see her there that she now let out a scream of her own.

'**Aaah!**' She clapped a hand to her chest.

'**Aaah!**' screamed Sparky, who was rather shocked by Mrs Smart's shock.

'What on earth...?' Mr Smart's voice sailed through the bedroom door, followed by Mr Smart himself.

'What's going on?' grumbled Stanley. He appeared on the landing and switched on the light. One pyjama

trouser leg seemed to have shuffled its way to just above his knee and got stuck.

'Mama!' shouted Sissy. 'Mama, Mama, Mama!'

'It's all right, Sissy,' called Mrs Smart. 'I'll be there in a moment. Stay in bed.'

Sissy didn't.

Mrs Smart recovered a little. 'Sparky!' she said. 'What are you doing? I thought you were a burglar! Why aren't you in bed? Are you still not feeling well? Why are you hanging about by the airing cupboard?'

Once again, Sparky Smart, the quickest thinker at Priory Park, needed to spring into action. But to be honest, Sparky had had to do so much quick thinking in the last few hours, her powers of quick thinkingness were beginning to wear a little thin.

'Well...' she began. 'I was in bed – and I was feeling really well, not cold or hot or anything – when... I thought I heard something.'

Mrs Smart's eyes went wide. 'A scream?' She turned to Mr Smart with a look of triumph. 'There you are, you see, I told you I heard a scream.'

'No, it wasn't a scream,' said Sparky quickly. She could imagine Mrs Smart rushing to phone the police, and the police arriving in next to no time, to find no sign of a burglar or, indeed, any sort of break-in. Then there'd be questions asked!

'No...' said Sparky, 'it definitely wasn't a scream, it was, erm... it was something *funny*...'

There was silence.

'Something *funny*?' said Stanley after a moment.

'Yes,' said Sparky. 'Most definitely something funny,

not something screamy.'

Mr Smart shook his head. 'Something funny... from where?' he asked.

All eyes were on Sparky.

'Well,' said Sparky, 'I can't be *completely* sure. I mean, I *was* in bed and everything. But I think... I think it might have been coming from the airing cupboard.'

All eyes darted to the airing cupboard.

'So,' said Mrs Smart, 'just to be completely clear – you were in bed and you heard something funny coming from inside the airing cupboard.'

Sparky nodded. 'Yes, that's it.'

Mr Smart looked as if he couldn't believe he'd been woken up in the middle of the night because there might be something funny in the airing cupboard. 'Right,' he said. 'Well, let's have a look then.'

He stepped towards the door.

'No!' Sparky stepped in front of it. 'You don't need to look. Because, erm... I've already looked, and there's nothing in there. Well, nothing that would make a funny sound anyway. So we may as well all go back to bed.'

Mrs Smart pressed her lips into a straight line.

'No, Sparky,' she said. 'We're all awake. We're all up. If you thought you heard something funny, the least we can do is let Dad have a look.'

'But there's nothing to look at,' said Sparky. *Please, please, PLEASE don't open the door!* she wished inside her head.

Mr Smart took another step forward.

Sparky didn't move. She looked at him and shook her head.

Mr Smart sighed and shook his head too. He reached around Sparky and placed a hand firmly on the handle of the door to the airing cupboard.

Still Sparky didn't move.

'Sparky!' he snapped.

Whenever Mr Smart snapped 'Sparky' or 'Stanley' like that, Sparky and Stanley knew their time had run out. Whatever it was they were doing that he wanted them to stop, now was the time. Whatever they *weren't* doing that he wanted them *to do*, now was also the time. (Sissy hadn't quite got the hang of this yet.)

Sparky's head drooped. 'Yes, Dad,' she said, and took a step sideways. All she could hope for now was that, when she'd tossed Grandad's slippers into the airing cupboard, they had landed somewhere out of sight.

Mr Smart threw open the door.

Starting at the top of the cupboard, he glanced from shelf to shelf. Stanley started from the top too. Mrs Smart, however, started from the floor.

If she'd let out a scream when she was surprised to see Sparky, it was nothing to the scream she let out now.

'AAAAAHH!'

Mrs Smart's eyes looked as though they might pop out of her head. One of them began a wild twitch, and she trembled from top to toe. She pointed a long, shaking finger.

'There! Right THERE!' she yelled. 'Rats! Giant rats! Don't let them out! Shut the door!'

As quick as a flash, Mr Smart slammed the door closed. He stared at Mrs Smart.

'Are you sure?' he said, 'Are you really sure? Are there

rats in there?'

Mrs Smart gave a frantic nod of her head. 'Two of them – didn't you see? How could you miss them? They're enormous!'

She held her hands wide apart to indicate their size. 'As big as this. Honestly, I'm not joking!'

Sparky wished the landing under her feet would open up and swallow her. Either that, or an alien space craft would appear and beam her on board as it flew past the window.

Mr Smart had had enough. Something about this whole situation just didn't feel right.

'This is daft,' he said. 'I've got to be up at six o'clock in the morning to run at least ten miles, and instead of getting a good night's sleep, what am I doing? I'm standing in front of an airing cupboard that might, or might not, be full of giant rats! I'm opening the door.'

'No!' cried Mrs Smart.

'No!' whispered Sparky.

'Yes!' said Mr Smart.

And he did.

Mrs Smart whisked Sissy into her arms and backed away.

Mr Smart's eyebrows shot up as he spotted the giant 'rats' on the cupboard floor.

He stood perfectly still – and so did they.

He inched forward, little by little. Very slowly, he lowered himself down to get a better look.

'Hmm...' he said.

He reached into the cupboard.

'No!' screeched Mrs Smart. 'No, they'll have your hand off!'

The 'rats' didn't have Mr Smart's hand off. In fact, now that he'd pulled them out into the light and could see them better, they looked much less like rats and rather more like soggy guinea pigs.

Sparky's head drooped so far down, she wondered if it might actually fall off.

Sissy giggled. 'Uggy ippers,' she said.

* * * *

Mrs Smart rang Grandad's front doorbell. Sissy sat in the pushchair in front of her. Sparky stood a little way behind. She held a carrier bag and her head still drooped. It hadn't stopped drooping since the 'giant rat' incident. What was surprising was that this hadn't given her a sore neck.

Grandad's shape appeared behind the coloured glass in the front door as he came to open it.

'Don't worry, Sparky,' said Mrs Smart. 'Just tell the truth.'

'Well, good morning,' said Grandad.

He peered at Mrs Smart. Her eyes looked puffy and there were dark smudges underneath.

'Oh, dear,' he said. 'Bad night?'

'You could say that, yes,' said Mrs Smart. 'Shall we go in?'

They followed Grandad down the hall.

In the kitchen, Sparky was surprised to see that Grandad was wearing slippers. No socks still, but brown slippers that looked a bit faded, and not nearly as cosy as the ones he thought he had lost.

Grandad noticed Sparky look at his feet. He wriggled

his toes. 'An old pair,' he said. 'These are the slippers I had before I got my extra-special ones from Canada. Which, incidentally,' he added, 'still haven't turned up.'

'Yes, well,' said Mrs Smart, 'there's a story behind that. Sparky?'

Sparky couldn't look Grandad in the eye. But the tale had to be told, and she was the one who had to tell it.

Sparky now knew that when she found Sissy covering the extra-special slippers in honey, she should have told Grandad straight away. Instead, her quick thinking had jumped into action far too – well, quickly – and she'd ended up in a much stickier situation than the slippers.

As Sparky finished the story, she pulled the slippers, which were still very soggy, out of the carrier bag. Grandad's bushy eyebrows did a sort of wiggle. He reached out and took them.

'But, you see, Grandad,' Sparky said, 'all I really wanted to do was help. I didn't want you to see your extra-special slippers from Canada all covered in honey. I thought I could put it right and you'd never need to know. I'm sorry, Grandad. I know you probably won't ever want me to come and visit again.'

Grandad's eyes twinkled. He looked at Mrs Smart.

'Did you really think these were giant rats?' he said.

'Yes,' said Mrs Smart, 'as a matter of fact I did.'

Grandad couldn't help a chuckle.

'It's not funny, actually,' said Mrs Smart. 'They gave me the fright of my life.'

Grandad turned and put the soggy slippers on the side next to the sink.

'Come here, Sparky,' he said.

Sparky did as she was told. When she was close enough, Grandad put his arms around her and gave her a hug.

'The thing is,' he said, 'you were only trying to help, and you didn't deliberately drown my slippers. So, as far as you never visiting again' – and he gave Sparky an extra squeeze – 'I'd miss you to the moon and back.'

'So,' said Sparky, who still couldn't bring herself to look at Grandad, 'you don't hate me?'

'Of course I don't hate you!' said Grandad. 'You're welcome here any time. In any case,' he added, 'for one thing, now you've told me where my slippers had disappeared to, I know I'm not going potty – which is always a plus when you get to my age. And for another, I'm sure I can order another pair of extra-special slippers. But there'll only ever be one of you, Sparky.'

Sparky looked up into Grandad's kind face. It was quite a relief to lift her head after drooping it for so long.

'You see?' she said. 'I told you you're like God, Grandad. He always forgives people when they get things wrong too.'

'I'll always love you, Sparky,' said Grandad, **'whatever you do.'**

'I'll always love you too, Grandad,' said Sparky.

Grandad let her go. 'Now, then,' he said, 'who's for some ice cream with a drizzle of honey from my china pot?'

'Gizzle,' said Sissy.

Mrs Smart raised an eyebrow.

Sparky glanced at her. No, there wouldn't be ice cream and honey so soon after breakfast today.

But amazing things do happen, especially if you've been awake half the night and found giant rats in your airing cupboard.

'Sounds perfect,' said Mrs Smart. 'Why not?'

A dog for a day

The Smart family lived in one of a row of town houses along Priory Park. The houses weren't joined to each other. (Houses like that are called 'detached', if you want to know the proper name.)

They were all built of orangey-red brick. They each had a garage and a driveway, and a step up to the front door. And behind each one was a garden. The gardens weren't huge, but they were big enough for some grass, a small tree (the Smarts had a small pear tree), some flower beds, and a shed (again, quite small). When the washing wasn't hanging out to dry, there was also room for **one of Mr Smart's death-defying obstacle courses.**

What there *wasn't* room for, Mrs Smart had said, was a dog.

'But our dog wouldn't live in the garden,' Sparky would argue, 'it would live in the house with us.'

'Yes, but dogs like to go outside too,' Mrs Smart would reply. 'They like to wander around and have a good sniff. There isn't enough wandering space in our garden. And anyway, we hardly have enough room in our house for all of *us*. Where are we going to put a dog?'

'It could stay in my room. Sissy and me, we wouldn't mind.'

'No, Sparky.'

'But I want a dog more than anything.'

'Sabrina – no.'

In the house to the right-hand side of the Smarts' house lived Mr and Mrs Obi. Mr Obi worked in IT and Mr Smart always said how clever he was. Mr Smart got on very well with Mr Obi. Sometimes at the weekend, they would go running together.

When Mr and Mrs Obi moved in, they were very happy to have Stanley and Sparky living next door. (Sissy hadn't arrived yet.) They seemed to love children. In fact, they seemed to love them so much that, a few months ago, they had had one of their own – a little boy they had named Eric, after Mrs Obi's father.

Mrs Obi was an estate agent. She helped people to buy and sell their homes. She liked being an estate agent, but she was in no hurry to go back to work after she'd had baby Eric.

'If we can manage without the extra money,' she told Mrs Smart, 'I'd like to try to stay at home for a while. After all, Eric won't be a baby for long and I don't want to miss any of it.'

Mrs Smart was very good friends with Mrs Obi. They would have cups of tea together. And Mrs Smart liked it when Mrs Obi asked her for advice about anything to do with babies. But secretly, Mrs Smart did rather envy her neighbour. She would have liked to be able to stay at home with her family too.

In the house to the left-hand side of the Smarts' house lived Miss Clatworthy.

Miss Clatworthy had lived at Priory Park before the Smarts moved there. The first thing she'd said to Mr and Mrs Smart when she met them in the road on their moving-in day was, 'Oh. I see you have children.' The Smarts only had Stanley. Sparky hadn't been born yet. But still, Miss Clatworthy had sounded very disappointed.

Miss Clatworthy, who was now retired, didn't like children at all. Sparky thought this was very odd as she used to be the head teacher of a primary school.

'But you have to like children a little bit if you're a head teacher – don't you?' Sparky had asked her parents.

'She probably does,' said Mr Smart. 'Somewhere...

deep down inside.' But he didn't say it as if he believed it.

If Stanley and Sparky were out in their garden at the same time as Miss Clatworthy was out in her garden, they could hear her sigh and tut if they laughed or chattered too loudly. And if they were attempting an obstacle course with Mr Smart cheering them on, they couldn't help noticing how she would bang her windows closed to shut out the noise.

As for Sissy's crying when she was a baby, to Miss Clatworthy, it was unforgivable. Sparky had heard her talking on her mobile phone in the garden. 'It's impossible to get any peace at Priory Park these days,' she had said. 'Especially now next door have produced *another* one. At least they don't have a dog. I suppose that's one blessing.'

No, **it wasn't just children Miss Clatworthy didn't like**. It was dogs too.

She did, however, like cats. Miss Clatworthy had three cats. One was ginger, one was black and white and fluffy, and one was grey. Their names were Monday, Tuesday and Thursday (no, really), but the Smarts had no idea which one was which.

As a cat lover – and most definitely *not* a lover of dogs or children – Miss Clatworthy was in for some very bad news.

Sparky and Grandad just happened to walk past Mr and Mrs Obi's front gate one day, as Mr Obi lifted a small cardboard box out of the back of his car.

'Wait there,' Mr Obi said. 'I've got something to show you.'

Mr Obi walked towards them with the box. He lowered it down so that Sparky would be able to see inside.

‘Ohhhh!’ Sparky couldn’t believe her eyes.

Inside the box was the tiniest puppy she had ever seen in her life. It was so tiny that, at first, Sparky almost didn’t realise it was a puppy at all.

‘Meet Minnie,’ said Mr Obi. ‘She’s a Chihuahua. Isn’t she just the cutest?’

Sparky was so taken with Minnie’s cuteness that she nearly couldn’t speak. The tiny puppy had very short, white hair and huge eyes, and pointy ears that looked far too big for her head.

‘*So* cute!’ Sparky managed to say, after a moment.

'Can I pat her?'

'Of course you can,' said Mr Obi. He glanced at Grandad. 'You're welcome to pat her too, if you like.'

'If it were me,' Grandad twinkled, 'I'd call her Big Ears.'

Sparky was shocked. '**Grandad!**' she said. '**That's so rude!**'

Grandad chuckled and Mr Obi smiled. He looked almost as proud as he had the day he and Mrs Obi had brought Eric home from hospital for the first time.

'Of course,' Grandad said, 'you do realise we're never going to hear the end of it now. This little one' – he pointed a finger at Sparky's head – 'has been after having a puppy for ages.'

'Well,' said Mr Obi, 'you're welcome to come round and play with Minnie any time you like, Sparky.'

That was the moment when Mr Obi spotted Miss Clatworthy.

Miss Clatworthy had just wheeled her rubbish bin out onto the pavement ready for the rubbish to be collected. The bin men weren't actually due until the day after tomorrow, but Miss Clatworthy always put her bin out a day early to make completely sure they didn't miss it.

Miss Clatworthy glanced towards Mr Obi. He and Mrs Obi had been in her bad books ever since Eric had arrived.

Mr Obi waved. 'Come and see what we've got, Miss Clatworthy!' he called.

Miss Clatworthy really couldn't care less. She pointed over her shoulder and shook her head. 'I've left the oven on,' she said.

'Oh, come and see, Miss Clatworthy,' said Sparky. 'It's the most gorgeous little puppy in the whole world!'

It was only as she finished speaking that Sparky suddenly remembered, 'At least they don't have a dog. I suppose that's one blessing.'

Of course! Miss Clatworthy hated dogs!

'Actually,' Sparky called quickly, 'don't worry about it, Miss Clatworthy. You'd better go back to the oven.'

Miss Clatworthy's shoulders went stiff and she pursed her lips. Sparky imagined this was the way she used to look when she was a head teacher and a naughty child was sent to her office.

Oops, Sparky thought.

She had once asked Grandad if he thought God loved Miss Clatworthy.

'**God loves everyone,**' Grandad had said. 'You, me, everyone – whatever we're like and whatever we've done. He doesn't pick and choose. He sees all the good things in people too. He sees what's good and kind in Miss Clatworthy.'

Wow, Sparky had thought. She wasn't sure there was anything good and kind in Miss Clatworthy. *It must be very hard to be God.*

Miss Clatworthy didn't come over to look at the puppy. She turned sharply and walked back through her gate.

'I must take Minnie in,' said Mr Obi. 'I can't wait to see Eric's face when he sees her.'

'Eric's so lucky,' said Sparky. 'He gets to grow up with a puppy.'

Sparky was now sure of one thing. Their garden was exactly the same size as Mr and Mrs Obi's garden. And if Mr and Mrs Obi's garden wasn't too small for a dog to go wandering and sniffing in, that meant one thing and one thing only: Mrs Smart didn't want a dog because she hated dogs – just like Miss Clatworthy.

✿ ✿ ✿ ✿

'You're very quiet, Sparky,' Mrs Smart said, when the Smarts had all sat down for dinner. 'Is anything the matter?'

'I quite like it,' said Stanley. 'It makes a nice change.'

'And who cares what *you* think?' said Sparky. 'You want to be a weather person, and since when did anyone ever care what weather people say? They're always wrong!'

'Sparky!' said Mr Smart. 'That's enough, thank you very much. What's the problem?'

Grandad had stayed for dinner. 'I think,' he said, 'it's probably got something to do with the new puppy next door.'

'What new puppy?' said Stanley. 'I didn't know there was a new puppy. Which side? Not Miss Clatworthy?'

'Of course not,' said Sparky. 'Miss Clatworthy hates dogs, everyone knows that.'

'Does she?' said Mr Smart.

'Does she?' said Mrs Smart.

Sparky raised her eyes.

'She does indeed,' said Grandad.

'So the Obis have got a puppy, have they?' said Mrs Smart. 'And a baby who's only a few months old too. Well, I don't envy them that.'

Sparky pulled a face. 'That's because you're like Miss Clatworthy and you hate dogs,' she said.

Mrs Smart looked surprised. 'No, I don't hate dogs,' she said. 'Whatever makes you say that?'

'Isn't it obvious?' said Sparky. '*You* said we couldn't have a dog because the garden isn't big enough. *You* said dogs like to wander around and have a good sniff, and there isn't enough wandering space in our garden. Well, our garden is exactly the same size as Mr and Mrs Obi's and they've got a puppy. So clearly, *they* like dogs and *you* don't.'

'Sabrina, do *not* speak to your mum like that,' said Mr Smart.

'It is a very tiny dog,' said Grandad.

'I *do* like dogs,' said Mrs Smart. 'I've never had one so I don't know much about looking after them, but I do like them.'

'They need food and cuddles and walks,' said Sparky. 'And sniffing space,' she added. 'What else is there to know?'

'There's probably a bit more to it than that,' said Mr Smart. 'They need training for a start. It's a lot of work training a dog.'

'How do you know?' said Sparky. 'Have you ever trained one?'

'Well, no, but – '

'Exactly,' said Sparky. 'It might not be that much work at all. Mr and Mrs Obi don't think it's too much work, otherwise they wouldn't have bought a puppy.'

'Mum,' said Stanley, 'please could you pass the pepper?'

'The thing is, Sparky,' said Mrs Smart, without passing the pepper, 'I have to go out to work and Mrs Obi doesn't. I know I'm here in the school holidays, but in termtime, I'm out. We're all out. And even when I'm here, I'm very busy. I just don't think it would be fair on a puppy. I don't have the time.'

Sparky pulled another face. 'I see,' she said. 'So it's not because the garden doesn't have enough sniffing space. It's because you're too busy.'

'Please could you pass the pepper, Mum?' repeated Stanley.

The pepper pot stayed where it was.

'It's both,' said Mum. 'The garden isn't all that big and I always have so much to do.'

'But you see,' Sparky went on, '*I* could look after our dog. You and Dad wouldn't have to do anything. I could feed it and take it for walks. I could play with it. I'm sure I could train it too. I tell Sissy what to do sometimes, and sometimes she even does what I say.'

'But you're like Mum,' said Grandad. 'You're out at school all week. And who's going to look after it then?'

'Well...' Sparky said. 'I've been thinking about that and I suppose...' she said, 'I suppose *you* could, Grandad.'

Grandad's bushy eyebrows bounced up. 'Oh, could I indeed?' he said. 'So, that's the plan. Get Grandad to do it.'

'Oh, but you'd love it, Grandad, I know you would!' said Sparky.

Mr Smart shook his head. 'I'm sure Grandad has plenty to do without looking after a dog as well. He gives up enough of his time helping us out with you three.'

There was silence. A rather cross, uncomfortable silence.

'Well,' said Sparky, 'just so you know, you won't be seeing me so much anymore. I'm going to be spending a lot more time round at Mr and Mrs Obi's, so that I can be with the puppy.'

'Hip, hip hooray,' said Stanley. 'Erm... pepper?'

'Oh, really?' said Mrs Smart. 'And I wonder what Mr and Mrs Obi will have to say about that.'

Sparky folded her arms with a look of triumph. 'Actually, Mr Obi said I could go round and play with her whenever I want.'

'Right,' said Mrs Smart.

'Right,' said Mr Smart.

'Could somebody *please* pass me the pepper?' said Stanley.

'Pep-pep,' said Sissy.

Grandad nudged Stanley's elbow. 'If I were you,' he said, 'I'd just go and get it yourself.'

* * * *

One Friday evening a few weeks later, there was a ring at the Smarts' front doorbell.

Sissy had just gone to bed. Stanley was in his bedroom finding out about the weather in South East Asia on his laptop. Mr Smart was out at a meeting about converting the old launderette into a new mini keep-fit centre, and Mrs Smart was on a lengthy phone call with Auntie Bella.

'Uh-oh, this could take ages,' Mrs Smart had said when her mobile rang. 'You know what Auntie Bella's like when she gets going.'

So far, Mrs Smart had been on the phone for three quarters of an hour.

So when the doorbell rang, it was Sparky who answered. She opened the front door to find Mrs Obi on the doorstep.

'Hello, Mrs Obi,' Sparky said.

'Hello, Sparky,' said Mrs Obi, 'is your mum around?'

'She's on the phone to Auntie Bella, and it could take ages,' Sparky said.

'Oh,' said Mrs Obi. She looked disappointed. 'I just wanted to ask her something. A favour really. **Quite a big favour.**'

'Well,' said Sparky, 'you could ask me and then I could ask her when she's off the phone. And then she can text you the answer.'

'Brilliant idea,' said Mrs Obi. 'You're not called Sparky for nothing, are you?'

Sparky beamed. 'So, how can we help you?' she asked, in the sparkiest way she could.

'What it is,' said Mrs Obi, 'is that my mum has just come out of hospital.'

'Oh, dear,' said Sparky.

'No, it was nothing serious,' said Mrs Obi, 'and she's absolutely fine. But I really want to go and see her tomorrow. You know, just to check everything's all right and she's got what she needs. My brother lives not far away so he's keeping an eye on her, but I really want to see her too.'

Sparky nodded. 'That's what I'd want to do,' she said.

'The trouble is that Mr Obi is going on a course tomorrow, so he can't be at home,' Mrs Obi continued. 'Now, I can take Eric. That's not a problem at all and my mum will love to see him. But – my mum has allergies. Quite terrible allergies. You've never known sneezing fits like them. So, what I can't take is Minnie.'

'Oh,' said Sparky. 'Can you be allergic to dogs?'

'Oh, yes,' said Mrs Obi. 'It's the hair. Pet hair in general isn't good if you've got allergies.'

'I see,' said Sparky. Her eyes grew just a little bit wider. She had quite a good idea about what Mrs Obi was going to say next.

'So, what I wondered,' Mrs Obi said, 'and I know it's a big thing to ask, and I quite understand if your mum wants to say no... What I wondered is if Minnie could possibly come to you tomorrow. Just for the day, of course. I'll be back in the evening and I'll pop round and pick her up as soon as I get home.'

Sparky's mouth fell open. She tried to stop it but it happened anyway.

'If you could ask your mum when she's off the phone, and then if she could text me as soon as possible,' said Mrs Obi, 'that would be so helpful. Then I'll know what I'm doing.'

'It'll be fine.' Sparky had said the words almost before she knew what she was doing.

'Aw,' said Mrs Obi. 'You're such a sweetie, Sparky. But just ask your mum and I'll wait for her text.'

'No, really,' said Sparky, 'it'll be fine. We're not doing anything tomorrow. And Mum'll love it. We might get a dog ourselves one day,' she added. 'So it'll be good practice.'

Sparky could hardly believe what was coming out of her own mouth. But here she was, with the chance to look after Minnie for a whole day, and nothing in the world would make her miss it.

'Besides,' she said, 'Mum's going to be on the phone for ages. Ages and ages. So it'll be ages and ages before she can text. And anyway, you need someone to help out. And they're always saying at church how important it is to help each other out. And Mum's always saying she wishes she could help people more, but she doesn't have time.'

'Well...' said Mrs Obi. 'I mean, if you're really sure. It means I could go now and let Mum know I'm coming, and get myself and Eric organised.'

'I'm really, *really* sure,' said Sparky. 'And Mum will be really, *really* sure, too, when I tell her.'

Of course, when Sparky said, 'when I tell her', she actually had no intention of telling Mrs Smart anything. Mrs Smart would probably come up with at least ten reasons why they couldn't have a dog for a day. Sparky imagined that Mrs Smart would rather have Eric for the day than Minnie.

No, no. Looking after Minnie would just have to be one BIG secret.

'You're amazing, Sparky!' said Mrs Obi. 'Thank you so much. No special instructions really. Minnie's very good and she's just about house-trained now, so there shouldn't be any accidents.'

A frown crossed Sparky's face. 'Accidents?' she said.

Mrs Obi smiled. 'She shouldn't leave you a little wee on the floor,' she said.

'Ohh!' said Sparky, and she smiled too. She was glad to hear this. If no one else knew there was a dog in the house, a little wee on the floor might be quite hard to explain.

'I'll get her stuff together – her cushion and her toys, and some food,' said Mrs Obi, 'and I'll drop it all round when I bring her first thing tomorrow morning.'

'Uh, no!' said Sparky. It came out more sharply than she meant it to.

Mrs Obi looked taken aback.

'I mean, don't worry about that. I'll come and get her,' said Sparky. 'And all her stuff. It's just... well, Mum quite often likes to have a lie-in on a Saturday. And it would mean you wouldn't have to disturb her.'

'You are such a thoughtful girl, Sparky,' said Mrs Obi. 'Your mum and dad are very lucky to have you.'

Sparky smiled. Although, if Mr and Mrs Smart knew she was planning to sneak a puppy into the house for a day, she wasn't completely sure how lucky they'd think they were.

Sparky closed the front door and went back into the lounge. She plonked herself down on the sofa and stared blankly at the TV. Someone was wittering on about how to bake a cake with no fat or sugar, but Sparky barely heard a word.

What had she done? Seriously – **what had she done?** The thing that had just happened – had it *actually* happened?

Sparky went back over the conversation in her head. Four times. Five times.

Yes. It had actually happened. Tomorrow, Sparky would be sneaking a tiny dog into their house and looking after it for the day, without letting the rest of the Smarts find out.

Sparky's mouth went dry. Oh, dear... if ever she needed to be quick thinking, it was now.

She started to put together a plan inside her head.

Number one – she would get up early. She would just have to hope that tomorrow was one of the mornings when Sissy didn't wake up even earlier.

Number two – she would get dressed downstairs so as not to make any sound that might wake Sissy up (or anyone else).

Number three – she would go round to Mrs Obi's at seven o'clock. Mrs Obi hadn't said exactly what time Sparky should go to collect Minnie, she'd just said first thing. Seven o'clock sounded like first thing to Sparky.

Number four – she would bring Minnie and all her stuff back to the house and...

And...

But that was it. That's where the plan ran out.

'I'll bring Minnie back here... and then what?'

Sparky lifted a thumb to her mouth and chewed at the nail as she went over various problems in her head. *What if I sneak her into the house and Mum and Dad are up? Or Sissy or Stanley? They'll see us. And even if they don't see us, I can't put Minnie in my bedroom because Sissy might still be in there. And there isn't anywhere else to hide her from Mum.*

Sparky chewed on her thumb nail so hard that a piece snapped off in her mouth and she had to fish it out with her fingers.

Then, suddenly, something clicked inside her brain, and the answer became clear.

It wasn't a perfect answer by any means. In fact, it probably couldn't have been any less perfect. But Sparky knew that if she was going to pull this off, it was the only way.

She couldn't do this on her own. She'd have to get Stanley to help her.

Mrs Smart walked into the lounge. 'Was that someone at the door?' She'd finished her long phone call with Auntie Bella.

'No,' said Sparky. Then, 'Well, yes,' she added. 'But they didn't want us. They wanted someone else.'

'Oh,' said Mrs Smart. 'Who did they want?'

'I don't know,' said Sparky. 'Anyway, I'm going up to see Stanley now.' And she left the room, as quickly as she could.

When Stanley was finding out things about the weather, he didn't like to be disturbed.

If anyone did disturb him, he'd get quite cross. 'This is my future,' he would say to whichever member of the

Smart family had done the disturbing. Even Sissy. 'This is important. I don't think you realise just how important this is. I'm going to be a weather person.'

'Revver nursnip,' Sissy would say.

Sparky knew Stanley would be cross if she knocked on his door. But she knocked on his door anyway.

'What?' snapped Stanley.

'May I talk to you, please, Stanley?' asked Sparky. She spoke as quietly as she could so that Mrs Smart wouldn't be able to hear. 'It's very important.'

'Well, this is my future,' Stanley said. 'This is important too. I don't think you realise just how important this is. I'm going to be a weather person.'

'And I don't think *you* realise just how important *this* is,' said Sparky. 'It's the most important thing ever in the history of important things. And the thing is, Stanley' – and Sparky put her mouth right up close to the door – **'I can't do it without you.'**

There was a pause.

The next instant, Stanley whipped his door open. He narrowed his eyes and peered hard at Sparky.

'What do you mean,' he said, 'you can't do it without me?'

'Exactly what I say,' said Sparky. She cast a furtive glance along the landing towards the staircase. 'Not out here, though. Please may I come in?'

There was another short pause. Then Stanley stood back to let Sparky into his room, and closed the door behind her.

'Come on then,' he said. He sounded impatient. 'What can't you do without me?'

'Erm...' Sparky began, 'well...'

‘Yes?’ said Stanley, and he made a tutting sound with his tongue.

‘All right,’ said Sparky, ‘but you’ve got to promise you’ll listen to the whole story before you flip your lid.’

‘I’m not promising anything,’ said Stanley.

‘Fine,’ said Sparky. She took a deep breath and said, as quickly as she could, **‘I need you to help me hide a dog.’**

Before Stanley could get a word in, Sparky went on to tell him all about her conversation with Mrs Obi.

She added in a few extra bits: ‘Mrs Obi is just *desperate* to go see her poor mum... She doesn’t have *anyone* else to turn to... And she *really* wants Minnie to come to us because I’ve visited her quite a few times and Minnie knows me.’

Sparky needed Stanley to understand that she honestly didn’t have any choice.

‘I see,’ said Stanley, ‘and I suppose this has got nothing to do with that fact that *you’re* desperate to have a dog so you’d do anything for the chance to look after Minnie?’

Sparky looked hurt. ‘Of course not,’ she said. ‘Mrs Obi needs our help and I want to be helpful.’

Stanley stared at her. ‘You’ve got to tell Mum,’ he said.

‘No!’ said Sparky. ‘Mum hates dogs, I know she does. She won’t want Minnie here, even for a day. And then I’ll have to tell Mrs Obi that we can’t have Minnie after all, and Mrs Obi will be *so* disappointed. No, Stanley. I’ll go round first thing in the morning to pick Minnie up, and then it’s up to us to hide her.’

Stanley shook his head. ‘It’s not up to me to do anything,’ he said. ‘This was your idea. You sort it out.’

'Oh, *please,* Stanley,' said Sparky. 'I can't do this on my own. For a start, I can't hide Minnie in *my* room, because it's Sissy's room too. I'll never be able to keep Sissy out of there all day. So we need to hide Minnie in *your* room.'

'We?' said Stanley. 'What's this *we* business? This has got nothing to do with me.'

Sparky ignored him. 'And then, of course,' she continued, 'I'll need you to be a distraction.'

'*What?*' said Stanley.

'A distraction,' said Sparky. 'I'll need you to distract Mum and Dad while I get Minnie into the house. Then I'll need you to distract them again each time I take Minnie out into the garden.'

Stanley shook his head. 'You've lost it, do you know that, Sparky?' he said. 'You're completely bonkers. Even if I say I'll help, it's never going to work. You know what Mum's like. She notices everything.'

'It *will* work,' Sparky insisted, '*if* we stick together. Oh, come on, Stanley, it'll be fun. We'll have a dog for a day! So, are you in?'

Stanley wasn't sure if he thought Sparky was incredibly stupid or incredibly brave. He sat down on the edge of his bed and folded his arms.

'Supposing I am "in", what's in it for me?'

Sparky had thought of that too. 'You can have the TV remote all to yourself for the next two weeks,' she said. 'And if Dad buys peanut butter next time he goes shopping, that's all yours too. I'll have cheese.'

Stanley nodded as he took this in. '*And,*' he added, 'if this all goes wrong and Mum finds out there's a dog in the house, it's got nothing to do with me, all right? I'm telling

Mum it was *your* idea and you made me do it. Deal?'

Sparky chewed her lip for a moment. 'Deal,' she said.

At half past six the next morning, Stanley crept into Sparky's room and woke her up. Stanley had set his alarm. Sparky couldn't set hers because it would wake Sissy.

Luckily, this wasn't one of Sissy's early wake-ups. Sparky was able to slide out of bed, grab her clothes and head downstairs without disturbing her.

At seven o'clock, Sparky slipped out through the front door and went to collect Minnie. She'd left Stanley on 'distraction' duty. If there was any sound or movement from either Sissy or Mr and Mrs Smart, Stanley was ready with a weather forecast. Odd, you might think, but Mr and Mrs Smart knew how serious Stanley was about being a weather person. If he tried out a weather forecast on them, he was fairly sure they'd sit still and listen to it. Whether they wanted to or not.

Sissy would hardly understand a word. But she loved making rain noises. So as long as Stanley's forecast was full of rainy weather and he let her join in with the sound effects, he knew he could keep her in her room.

Happily, no one woke up while Sparky was next door. Mrs Obi was a little surprised to see her quite so early, but she had everything packed and ready for Minnie's day out.

'Why don't I help you carry everything round?' said Mrs Obi. 'I can thank your mum for being so kind too.'

'You don't have to,' said Sparky. 'I've already said thank you. I'll say thank you again, if you like. Besides, knowing Mum, if she's not lying in, she'll probably be on the phone now.'

Mrs Obi looked surprised. 'At seven o'clock in the morning?'

'Oh, yes,' said Sparky. 'Sometimes Mum can be on the phone all weekend.'

Minnie wasn't at all happy about leaving Mrs Obi. She kept looking back as Sparky walked her to the Obis' gate on her lead. And when they reached the gate, she tried to pull the other way and run back to the house.

'Aw, it's all right, Minnie,' said Mrs Obi. She looked a bit upset too. 'I'll be back very soon. Sparky will look after you.'

She waved at the tiny puppy and blew kisses.

But Minnie wasn't going anywhere. She planted her four paws firmly on the driveway and refused to move.

'Come on, Minnie,' said Sparky. 'You're coming with me today. We're going to have so much fun.'

It was obvious Minnie didn't think it would be fun at all.

'Hold on,' said Mrs Obi, 'I'll just fetch my shoes and bring her round. She'll go if I come too.'

Naturally, Mrs Obi bringing Minnie round was the last thing in the world Sparky wanted.

'No, no!' Sparky said. 'I can do it. I really can. Bye bye, Mrs Obi. Have a lovely day with your mum.'

With that she called, 'Minnie!' in an encouraging sort of way and pulled firmly on Minnie's lead. Minnie started to move – although her legs didn't. Because she was so small, Sparky found she could quite easily pull her gently along in short bursts.

At last, Sparky managed to get Minnie out of the Obis'

gate, in through her own gate, and up to the front step. But it all took much longer than she thought it would.

Slowly, cautiously, Sparky pushed open the front door. The actual pushing had to happen with her foot as she had no free hands. One held Minnie's bag of food and toys; the other held Minnie's lead, with an obstinate Minnie on the other end.

The first thing Sparky looked for was Stanley. Stanley

was still waiting for her at the top of the stairs, just as she'd told him to. He gave her a quick thumbs up and she breathed a sigh of relief. *Phew! All clear...*

Now all Sparky had to do was get Minnie up to Stanley's bedroom. Simple.

Minnie, however, had her own ideas. Not only did she not want to leave Mrs Obi, she didn't want to step inside Sparky's house either. After all, what was this place? She'd never been there before. She didn't like the look of it, and when she sniffed, she certainly didn't like the smell of it.

So, Minnie stopped at the foot of the front step and wouldn't move.

Sparky gave her lead a tug. 'Come on, Minnie,' she whispered. 'We've got to get inside.'

Still, Minnie didn't move.

Sparky tried again. 'Minnie, we really have to go in. You'll like it. You will, honestly.'

Minnie stared at Sparky with her huge brown eyes. Sparky gave her a big, beaming smile. And Minnie sat down.

'No!' hissed Sparky. 'No, Minnie, you can't stay here. We have to go in.' She glanced up at Stanley who still stood at the top of the stairs.

'Pick her up,' Stanley mouthed. He couldn't say anything out loud for fear of being heard.

'What?' whispered Sparky.

Stanley rolled his eyes. 'Pick her up!' he mouthed again. This time, he mimed picking something up with both hands.

'Ohh!' whispered Sparky. 'Good idea.'

As she already had Minnie's bag of things in one hand, Sparky only had one hand free for the picking up. She managed this quite easily as Minnie was so tiny. What she didn't expect was Minnie's little whimper.

Actually, it wasn't so little. It was more like a howl, and it sounded as if it was coming from a dog that was much, much bigger. Minnie didn't want to be picked up, and she made very sure that Sparky knew it.

'Sssh! Sssh – it's all right, Minnie,' Sparky whispered. 'Everything's all right.'

The howl didn't stop.

At the top of the stairs, Stanley looked panic-stricken.

'Put her down!' he mouthed. 'Put her down!' His hands did a quick mime of dropping something to the floor.

Sparky quickly put the tiny dog back down on the ground. Straightaway, the howl stopped.

Stanley's heart thudded. He glanced towards Mr and Mrs Smart's bedroom door. He listened. But all seemed to be quiet. And he gave Sparky another thumbs up.

The fact that Mr and Mrs Smart were still asleep was good news.

The fact that Sparky couldn't seem to get Minnie inside the house quietly, was bad news – with a capital B-N.

And the news was about to get worse.

'Oggy!'

Stanley almost jumped out of his skin. He'd been so keen not to wake up Mr and Mrs Smart that, for the moment, he'd forgotten about Sissy. Sissy now stood next to Stanley at the top of the stairs.

Through the open door, Sissy could just see Minnie peeping over the front step. Sissy pointed. She jiggled her knees in excitement.

'Oggy!' she said again and giggled. 'Oggy, oggy!'

Fortunately, the stair gate meant that Sissy couldn't scramble downstairs to give Minnie one of her 'special' hugs. (Sissy had a particular way of hugging her favourite cuddly toys. She would wrap her arms around their necks – not their tummies – and give them a tight squeeze. The thought of her trying to hug Minnie in the same way didn't bear thinking about.)

*Un*fortunately, as Sissy couldn't get downstairs, she kept jiggling and giggling, and saying, 'Oggy!' over and over *and over* again.

This, in turn, meant that it was only a matter of seconds before Mrs Smart woke up.

'Sissy,' Mrs Smart mumbled, still mostly asleep. 'Sissy, what is it? Come here.'

'Oggy!' said Sissy. 'Parky got oggy! Parky got lully oggy!'

'Sissy...' Mr Smart was awake now too. 'Come on, sweetheart, come and see us.'

Sparky's eyes bulged in horror. Stanley looked rather horrified himself.

'Now what?' he mouthed.

'Erm... garden!' hissed Sparky. 'Come and find me when it's all clear again!'

'When it's all clear again?' Stanley mouthed. 'When is it ever going to be all clear now? Everyone's awake!'

But Sparky took no notice. She'd already sprung into action.

She stepped backwards out of the house and shut the front door. Then, she scooped Minnie up with her one free hand. Instantly, Minnie opened her mouth and began to howl.

As quickly as she could, Sparky crossed the drive and ran down the side of the house to the back gate.

The second they were out of sight, Sparky put Minnie down again.

The noise Minnie was making stopped immediately.

Sadly, so did Minnie. Once again, she planted her paws on the ground and wouldn't budge.

'Oh, come *on*, Minnie, this isn't funny,' said Sparky.

Gently, carefully, she pulled on the lead and managed to get Minnie as far as the gate. She clicked the latch, pushed the gate open, and gently, carefully, pulled Minnie through into the garden.

Minnie's huge brown eyes continued to stare at Sparky. Only now, they looked less worried and more cross.

'Don't look at me like that,' said Sparky. 'I'm trying to help.'

The only place to hide in the garden was round the back of the shed. There was a small space there between the shed and the hedge that separated the Smarts' garden from Miss Clatworthy's garden.

Sparky had used it as a hiding place quite a few times. Stanley was the only one who ever found her there, so she felt it would be safe. Also, when Stanley wanted to give her the all clear so that she could take Minnie into the house, he'd know where to look for her.

Of course, the only way Sparky could get Minnie behind the shed was to carry her – which meant rather a lot of howling and yowling was involved. Still, once they were there, at least they couldn't be seen.

'I definitely heard a dog crying. There must be a dog in the garden.'

Sparky froze.

Mrs Smart had just stepped outside the back door. 'It was a dog, I know it was. Or, if it wasn't a dog,' she added, 'it sounded more like a dog than most dogs.'

'No, it wasn't a dog,' said Stanley.

He'd followed Mrs Smart into the garden. He knew Sparky was out there. He also knew exactly where she'd be hiding.

Sparky couldn't see Stanley, but she could hear him as he tried to cover up the panic in his voice.

'It truly wasn't a dog,' he said. 'It was me. Listen...'

Stanley cleared his throat.

'**Oowoowoowoowooo!**' he howled.

Sparky was impressed. Stanley really did sound remarkably like Minnie.

Minnie seemed to think so too. She frowned (if dogs can frown) and pricked up her huge, pointy ears.

'That's nothing like what I heard,' said Mrs Smart.

'It is,' Stanley insisted. 'It was, it was me. Oowoowoowoowooo!' he howled again, just to make the point.

'But, Stanley,' said Mrs Smart, 'if it *was* you – and I'm not convinced it was – why would you make such a terrible racket? On a Saturday morning? Why would you wake me and Dad up – not to mention Sissy? Apart from anything else,' she went on, 'it's just not like you to be so... silly. I mean, why would you want to sound like a dog?'

There was a pause.

Stanley forced a smile. 'I thought it would make a

change from doing the weather forecast,' he said.

This made Sparky want to giggle.

She might have giggled, too, if what happened next, hadn't happened.

One of Miss Clatworthy's cats – Monday, Tuesday or Thursday, Sparky didn't know which, but it was the black-and-white-and-fluffy one – suddenly appeared in Miss Clatworthy's garden, just the other side of the hedge.

The hedge here was quite thin. There was actually a hole in it, close to the ground. So it was very easy to see through to the other side. That's why Mrs Smart had thought it would be a good place to put the shed. It would stop Miss Clatworthy from spying on them. Spying on neighbours did seem like something Miss Clatworthy would do, given half a chance.

If Sparky had been looking through the hedge at the time, she would have spotted the cat before Minnie did. As it was, she didn't realise it was there until it was too late.

Minnie started to bark. It was a funny, high-pitched, squeaky sound. Not very scary at all, but enough to startle the cat, who shot off across Miss Clatworthy's lawn.

Minnie, however, wasn't about to let it go. This was probably the most exciting thing to have happened since she'd arrived at Priory Park.

She tugged hard at her lead. Even though Sparky was taken off guard, she was able to hold on to her easily. Minnie hardly weighed a thing. It was a bit like being pulled by a budgie. But, that wasn't the end of it.

Oh, no. Minnie was far cleverer than she looked.

The little dog did a quick shuffle and a twist, followed

by a backwards scrabble. Moments later, she had slipped out of her collar, dived through the hole in the hedge, and was chasing Miss Clatworthy's black-and-white-and-fluffy cat across Miss Clatworthy's grass.

Sparky stared in dismay at the empty lead that still dangled from her hand. *Nooo!* she screamed in her head.

Mrs Smart had heard the barking. (We'll call it 'barking' but actually, if Stanley had barked, he would have sounded more like a dog than Minnie.)

She ran towards the shed.

Stanley ran after her. 'It was me!' he said. 'It was me! Woof! Woof, woof, WOOF!'

Too late.

Mrs Smart already stood, hands on her hips, glaring round the back of the shed.

'**Sabrina Smart,**' she said. '**Come out of there this minute.**'

Sparky looked at the hole in the hedge. She looked back at Mrs Smart.

'I will come out,' she said. 'There's just one thing I've got to do first.'

With that, she crouched down and scrabbled her way into Miss Clatworthy's garden, before Mrs Smart had the chance to stop her.

'Sabrina!' shrieked Mrs Smart. 'Sabrina, come here right now!'

'What is it?' Mr Smart appeared in the back doorway. 'What on earth's going on?'

Sissy pushed past him. 'Oggy!' she called. 'Parky got oggy!'

Once on the other side of the hedge, Sparky ran into

the middle of Miss Clatworthy's lawn. Where was Minnie? Sparky's head turned left, right and left again, so quickly she almost felt dizzy. But there was no sign of a small, white dog.

Suddenly, a cat shot past her leg. Not the black-and-white-and-fluffy one this time. The cat that now hurtled towards the house was ginger.

Seconds later, Minnie appeared and raced after it.

'Minnie! Minnie!' Sparky yelled.

Minnie took no notice, so Sparky began to run again. She chased the tiny dog at full speed towards the back door of the house.

The ginger cat, a little way ahead of Minnie, reached the door first and took a flying leap through the cat flap. It probably thought it had escaped.

But although cat flaps are for cats (that's why they're called 'cat' flaps), they are also the perfect size for small Chihuahua puppies. This particular small Chihuahua puppy could see that at once.

'Minnie, no!'

Minnie jumped. Her little legs paddled backwards and forwards in mid-air. The cat flap flapped – and the little dog disappeared.

The next thing Sparky heard was a scream.

A loud scream.

A loud, very long, and really quite horrifying scream.

The scream came from Miss Clatworthy.

It was followed by a yell that sent a shiver down Sparky's spine. '**WHAT ON EARTH ARE YOU DOING IN MY HOUSE?**'

Who would have thought Miss Clatworthy had such a loud voice?

A few moments later, Miss Clatworthy appeared behind the glass in the back door.

When she spotted Sparky, her eyes glittered with fury. Slowly she raised a hand. In the hand, she held Minnie by the scruff of her neck. Minnie wriggled and kicked and howled, but there was no escape.

Uh oh...

Sparky's fingers twisted together.

This was bad. This was very bad. This was possibly one of the worst things that had ever happened. Worse even than the drowning of Grandad's sticky slippers.

What should Sparky do in such a situation? Should she smile? Should she wave?

Should she drop into a curtsy (she still remembered how to do those from ballet)?

Sparky had no clue. She thought perhaps the curtsy idea was quite a good one. But in the end, she just stood still and waited for whatever was going to happen, to happen.

Miss Clatworthy opened her back door. She fixed Sparky with the grimmest of grim stares.

Sparky tried a smile. 'Erm...' she gulped. 'Good morning, Miss Clatworthy... Would you like me to take Minnie now?'

Miss Clatworthy didn't move. She didn't speak. She didn't even blink. It seemed to Sparky that she didn't blink for ages. For so long, in fact, that Sparky found herself wondering if Miss Clatworthy was actually some terrifying, dog-hating, non-blinking monster in a human body...

Finally, at long last, Monster Clatworthy held Minnie

out towards Sparky. It was as if the small dog was the most revolting thing she had ever touched in her life.

Sparky reached out and took her. To Sparky's surprise, Minnie stopped howling instantly. Perhaps she realised Sparky's were far safer hands to find herself in than Miss Clatworthy's.

'Take IT away and get out of my garden,' Miss Clatworthy said. Her face was so stiff with fury that her lips barely moved. 'And if IT ever chases one of my cats again, don't expect to get IT back in one piece!'

Before Sparky could say, 'Yes, Miss Clatworthy. Thank you very much, Miss Clatworthy. I'm really very sorry, Miss Clatworthy', Miss Clatworthy had spun round and disappeared back into her house.

Sparky shuddered. She looked at Minnie. She swallowed hard.

Yes, she'd rescued Minnie from the fury on this side of the hedge. Now she had to face the fury on the other side.

Mrs Smart still stood by the shed with her hands on her hips. Mr Smart stood next to her. Stanley seemed to have slapped his hands on his head in an 'oh, help' sort of way. Sissy ran around the garden, barking.

When Sissy saw Sparky appear from behind the shed with Minnie, she stopped barking and started to shout, 'Oggy! Give oggy speshul cuggle!'

Sparky stood in front of Mr and Mrs Smart and Stanley. Nobody spoke. Except Sissy, of course, who kept saying, 'Give oggy me.'

Sparky felt as though she *should* say something. But, really and truly, she didn't know what to say. So saying nothing seemed like the better option.

Just as Mrs Smart opened her mouth and was about to speak, there was a knock at the back gate.

'Hello? Anyone there?' It sounded very much like Mr Obi.

It *was* Mr Obi.

'I've been ringing the front doorbell,' he called, 'but as there was no answer, I've come round the back. Hope that's all right.'

Mrs Smart closed her mouth. She looked at Mr Smart who shook his head and threw up his hands. Then he marched over to the gate and opened it.

'Morning,' said Mr Obi. 'Sorry, didn't mean to catch you in your jim jams.'

Mr Smart glanced down at his pyjamas then back at Mr Obi. 'No problem,' he said.

'Anyway, it's good news,' said Mr Obi.

'Is it?' said Mr Smart.

'My course has been cancelled,' said Mr Obi. 'I just got a call. I don't have to go to Bristol after all. That means I'm home today.'

'Right,' said Mr Smart. 'Well, that's... jolly good, isn't it?'

He forced a smile, even though he hadn't a clue what Mr Obi was talking about.

Mr Obi glanced across at Minnie, still in Sparky's arms.

'So, I've come to collect this little one,' he said. He gave Minnie a big, beaming smile. 'You know, I can't tell you how grateful we are to you for saying you'd have her today. Really, *really* kind of you. All of you. But now we don't need to trouble you because I'm at home. So I'll take her off your hands,' he added, 'and let you go and, erm... get dressed.'

Mr Smart looked at Mrs Smart. Mrs Smart still stood

by the shed. She gazed at Mr Obi as if he had just arrived from a different planet.

Mr Obi marched towards Sparky. As soon as Minnie had seen him, she'd begun to squirm and whimper in Sparky's arms. The moment Mr Obi was close enough, she hurled herself towards him.

'Whoops!' said Mr Obi. He took another quick step forward and caught her. His face then got very wet as Minnie wouldn't stop licking it.

'Stop that, you dafty,' he said. Minnie didn't stop and Mr Obi didn't seem to mind.

'Oh,' said Sparky. 'You'll need this too.' She disappeared round the back of the shed and returned with the bag of Minnie's bits and pieces.

'Thank you, Sparky,' said Mr Obi. 'And next time we need a dog-sitter, maybe you won't mind if we call on you again.'

Sparky laughed. At least, she tried to laugh. It sounded more as though she had hiccups.

'Bye then, all,' said Mr Obi. 'I'll leave you to your weekend.'

Mr and Mrs Smart, Stanley and Sparky raised their hands and gave a little wave.

Sissy ran around singing, 'Bye to oggy, oggy bye – bye to oggy, oggy bye!'

Mr Smart shut the gate behind Mr Obi, then turned and stared hard at Sparky. Mrs Smart's eye twitched furiously.

Sparky honestly wasn't sure whether she should shrink or melt.

'**Oh, Sabrina Smart,**' said Mrs Smart, in a quiet, sing-song voice. '**This had better be good...**'

Sparky knocked on Stanley's bedroom door.

'You can come in as long as you're not Sparky,' Stanley said.

Sparky sighed. 'Please, Stanley,' she said. 'I just want to talk to you.'

'Well, I don't want to talk to you. And why should I listen to anything you've got to say anyway? I listened to you last night and look at the mess *that* got me into.'

'I know,' said Sparky. 'And I'm really sorry.'

'So you should be,' said Stanley.

Sparky was glad that saying sorry to God wasn't as hard as saying sorry to Stanley. She knew that when she said sorry to God, as long as she meant it, God forgave her. **God loved her.**

God had forgiven her for the lies she'd told to Mrs Obi so that she could have a dog for a day. He'd forgiven her for not being honest with Mr and Mrs Smart.

God had even forgiven her for dragging Stanley into it, which meant he'd ended up telling lies too.

But for all she knew, Stanley would *never* forgive her.

'You can still have the TV remote all to yourself for the next two weeks,' Sparky said.

No answer.

'And if Dad buys peanut butter,' she added, 'you can still have the whole jar.'

No answer.

'Oh, please, Stanley, don't hate me. I know I'm an idiot. I know I did the wrong thing. But I'm going to try really, really hard to do the right thing from now on. I've asked

God to help me,' said Sparky, 'and He will. That's what Dad says and Dad's always right about God.'

There was another pause. The door to Stanley's bedroom opened.

'I'm having the TV remote for the next *three* weeks,' he said.

Sparky nodded.

'And I'm have the next *two* jars of peanut butter.'

Sparky nodded again.

Stanley folded his arms and looked at her. 'I tell you what, though,' he said, and his mouth suddenly stretched into a huge grin, 'I'd love to have seen Miss Clatworthy's face when Minnie shot through the cat flap.'

Sparky blinked at him. Her mouth began to grin too.

'It was terrifying!' she said. 'It was like this...'

Sparky made a face that she thought might look something like Miss Clatworthy's, and she stared hard with wide monster eyes.

Stanley giggled. 'Hold on,' he said. 'I want a photo.'

When Sparky saw her face on Stanley's phone, she laughed. She laughed and laughed.

She didn't look much like Monster Clatworthy, but it didn't matter. She and Stanley? They were friends again.

Join the Smart family and the other residents of Priory Park for more fun!

THE CRINKLY COUSINS AND OTHER MISHAPS
ISBN 9781838581497

THE PURRING WOMBAT AND OTHER MISADVENTURES
ISBN 9781838581503

THE WRONG TOILET AND OTHER DISASTERS
ISBN 9781838581510

THE SCHOOL FETE FIASCO AND OTHER CALAMITIES
ISBN 9781838581527

SHIPWRECKED AT THE LIBRARY AND OTHER EXPLOITS
ISBN 9781838581534

GRANDAD JELLY LEGS AND OTHER ESCAPADES
ISBN 9781838581541

All of the books in the **Spark Smart from Priory Park** series are available from **kevinmayhew.com** or from your local Christian bookshop